Blessed Are the Addicts

Blessed Are the Addicts

*The Spiritual Side of
Alcoholism, Addiction, and Recovery*

John A. Martin

HarperSanFrancisco
A Division of HarperCollinsPublishers

FIRST HARPERCOLLINS PAPERBACK EDITION

Reprinted by arrangement with Villard Books, a division of Random House,
Inc.

Library of Congress Cataloging-in-Publication Data

Martin, John A.
    Blessed are the addicts : the spiritual side of alcoholism,
    addiction, and recovery / John A. Martin. — 1st HarperCollins pbk.
    ed.
        p.   cm.
    Originally published: New York : Villard Books, 1990.
    ISBN 0-06-250556-4 (alk. paper)
    1. Alcoholics—Religious life.   2. Narcotic addicts—Religious
life.   3. Alcoholism—Religious aspects.   4. Drug abuse—Religious
aspects.   I. Title.
[BV4596.A48M35   1992]
362.29′186—dc20   91–55471
                                                                      CIP

---

91   92   93   94   95   FAIR   10   9   8   7   6   5   4   3   2   1

This edition is printed on acid-free paper that meets the American National
Standards Institute Z39.48 Standard.

To my mother and father, Irene and Arthur Martin
To the People . . . who love life at whatever cost

Contents

	Preface	xi
1	A Spiritual Disease	3
2	The Meaning of Spiritual	11
3	The Beginnings of Spiritual Addiction	18
4	The Discovery of the Drug	37
5	Spiritual Progression of the Disease	59
6	Birth of Spiritual Sobriety — Life	69
7	Instinct of Hope	74
8	Instinct of Faith	82
9	Spiritual Progression of Recovery	92
10	The Mystery of Mysteries	111
11	A Short Conclusion	119

Preface

I never wanted to write a book. Affluent societies have too many books. And, paradoxically, too many books produce too few avid readers, and still fewer books of note.

But something happened in my life. In the course of my own slow, painful, and certainly miraculous development, I was led to work with alcoholics and drug addicts.

As a child, my most vivid memory is the pain caused by my father's drinking. I didn't understand it at the time, but it remains the experience of my childhood years that is the most real and the most haunting, even to this day. Although my father is now deceased, I still cannot bring myself to call him an alcoholic. I do believe that if he were alive today, he would say it for himself.

He was a good man. An excellent provider, he loved me and, at all cost, wanted me to get an education. Setting his sights on a private preparatory school fifty miles from our home, he enrolled me there as a resident student.

A week into the school year, my father visited me, hoping to find that I liked it. When I informed him that I didn't want to stay, he was dismayed and asked me the reason. I told him that I couldn't be away from home and worry about his drinking at the same time. He told me to stay in school, because he wouldn't drink anymore. I was then fourteen years old. That very day my father stopped drinking, and remained sober until he died twenty-eight years later.

I went on to finish my education, and was ordained a Catholic priest in 1957. My first assignment was in the field of education. During the next thirteen years, I was to serve as a teacher of English, dean of students, and director of summer school. When the school closed in 1970, I accepted an offer to work in a Hispanic parish in New York City. This parish, located on a busy thoroughfare of Manhattan, was frequented by all kinds of people. It was here that I first encountered alcoholics and drug addicts in rather large numbers. I spoke with those who were only looking for money to maintain their habit; those who were so sick that they needed immediate care; those who were really looking for a way to stop drinking and/or drugging.

These alcoholics and drug addicts whom I met gave me my first education and taste for the field of addiction. It is they who propelled me, almost without previous thought or planning, to discover the world of detoxification centers and rehabilitation programs, where I helped to place many of them, and of twelve-step programs, such as Alcoholics Anonymous and Narcotics Anonymous, where I would bring them.

In time, I became familiar not only with the direct experience of addiction from the many addicts I continued to meet, but also with the professionals in the field—counselors, administrators of treatment facilities, nurses and doctors in hospitals, and directors of employment-assistance programs. I attended the Rutgers University School of Alcoholism and numerous workshops, conferences, and seminars on the subject of addiction.

I found myself spending most of my time with addicted people, who were coming in ever-growing numbers to the parish. Gradually, my strictly parish duties were becoming less appealing to me. A decision had to be made. Strangely enough, it was made for me.

In early 1983, I was approached by a twenty-year veteran in the field of alcoholism and drug addiction. In the course of our conversation, he mentioned how the spiritual element was greatly ignored by treatment models. This information sparked an immediate response in me. I went home, and within three days had produced an outline of a program of lectures dealing with the spiritual side of addiction and of recovery. Encouraged by my closest friends, I attempted to sell the idea and my program to treatment centers.

Within two months, I was hired by a treatment center caring for alcoholics and drug addicts. Since then and to this day, I have worked in various facilities where I give lectures on the spiritual part of the disease and of recovery. They have been and continue to be well received. In addition, I have become more and more convinced of the necessity to treat the spiritual, because it answers to a need that no other aspect of treatment directly addresses.

Out of that first encounter with addicts in the little parish that I served, my life changed, and events led me to do things that I would have never been able to predict. One of them is right now in your hand. I wrote a book.

I wrote it because I fell in love with every alcoholic and drug addict I ever met. It is a love that takes the form of deep compassion when one is aware of the horrendous pain caused by this disease. Spiritually, this love stirs one's soul; it makes one want to reach out and hug the suffering addict in the same way that one wants to feed the skin-stretched bodies of starving children with their oversized and pleading eyes that one sees in haunting photos. To begin to love an addicted person, one has first to catch him in his pain. Somehow that pain of life in the addict fosters the awareness of one's own deep pain. An identification is made, and love is born.

That love grows into a special joy when one accompanies the diseased person to health—to recovery. To experience the change in a person from addiction to recovery is to witness a miracle. In front of one's very eyes, the liar becomes the lover of truth, the thief becomes the trusted servant, the violent and destructive person becomes the peacemaker, the irresponsible man or woman becomes responsible, the uncaring becomes the lover of this world. How can one walk away from such a transformation? How can one come out of that experience not filled with love and admiration for the healing process as well as for the individual addicts whom one encounters?

That kind of love is compelling. It is a law unto itself. In writing this book, I am merely following the dictates of that love. Therefore, this book is about alcoholism and drug addiction.

The second half of our century has popularized the phenomenon we call addiction. In fact, our century seems to have discovered several addictions. We speak today, for example, of alcoholism, drug addiction, gambling, addiction to food, to sex, to people, to work, to feelings—maybe even in some cases to religion. I believe that in the next century we will discover thousands more.

Although this book focuses on alcoholism and drug addiction, everything that is said here can apply to all addictions. The reason is that all addictions are the same. On the outside, they have different manifestations and varied forms of expressions. When viewed from the inside, from their root, addictions are identical. In all forms of addiction, the pain, the inner experience, is the same, and the remedy is the same.

Without a doubt, I believe this book can be beneficial to all people. In considering life itself, one can suspect that maybe all people are addicted—that maybe all people have a way of evading the reality of life in more or less subtle forms. In the case of the alcoholic and the drug addict, the form is less subtle because these addictions become so physical and so visible that they are hard to deny or to conceal.

And thank God that there are addictions! For it is through the experience of addiction that one can become aware of the call of life. Through addiction, one is given the opportunity to wake up, to mature, to respond to that call in a positive and creative way. One can finally say a conscious yes to one's destiny and become one with oneself, one's world and one's God.

Before delving into the topic, I want to acknowledge all alcoholics and drug addicts whom I was graced to meet and know in the state of the disease as well as in the state of recovery. Also, I want to express a word of everlasting gratitude to the dear friends who encouraged me with their constant and proven love. Finally, a quiet prayer to the founders of Alcoholics Anonymous—Bill Wilson and Dr. Bob Smith. Their gift of the twelve-step recovery program was given not only for alcoholics, but for all the people of the world. This gift is not only given to recover from alcoholism, but, as events are proving, for the benefit of all addicted people. Finally, this gift is not only a way out of addiction, but it is a way into life. Viewed in that light, it might be said that somehow we are all in search and in need of this recovery.

Blessed Are the Addicts

1

A Spiritual Disease

MYSTERY FOREVER REMAINS a characteristic of addiction. Like all things of mystery, much is already known, and we hope that much more will be known in the future.

One thing generally agreed upon today by more and more professionals is a definition of addiction. It is a disease that is physical, mental, and spiritual.

To date, attention has mainly centered on the physical and the mental aspects of this disease. And validly so. As humans, we must first deal with what is most evident. And God knows that this disease does not disguise its presence. It distorts the valid feelings, crazes the sane mind, and ultimately kills the healthy body. A debt of gratitude is owed to the many people who so generously dedicate themselves to the research and to the healing of this fatal disease.

My purpose is to speak to the spiritual aspect of addiction. Though not immediately evident, I believe that this disease is mostly due not to a sick body, a crazy mind, or a deficient set of feelings, but rather to a certain dysfunction or, more accurately, to a disconnection of the human spirit. To make that statement is to plunge right into the thick of the mystery.

I used to say that this disease is 90 percent spiritual. I now say without any doubt that it is 100 percent spiritual. I don't believe anymore that there is such a thing as a spiritual component alongside a mental and physical component. I now believe that the disease is spiritual and includes a physical and mental aspect—all parts or expressions of the spiritual phenomenon at play. The beginning, the progression, the tragic end of this disease, are at the core spiritual, directly causing the harmful consequences we witness in the mind and body of the victim.

That is why this disease is time-consuming. In the case of suicide, a simple swallow of arsenic causes death in a short time. With addiction, the repeated ingestion of a drug by a diseased person takes time—sometimes years—to do its damage thoroughly. This scenario bears out the truth of those who say, "The spiritual is the first to go . . . and the last to come back." For certain, the spiritual—like life itself—operates in the framework of a process . . . never in the form of a fatal blow of an instant, such as in suicide.

I know that this disease isn't primarily physical. If it were, upon first experiencing an ill-effect, I would see a medical doctor, who, informed of my problem, would give me a prescription containing an antidote and say to me, "Take this twice a month, and the drug will not be harmful to you." If the antidote didn't yet exist, as in the case of some allergies like hay fever, for example, the doctor world merely inform me that the drug is the cause and that I should avoid it.

If this disease were only physical, I, the patient, upon hearing the doctor speak, would feel some anger and revolt at the thought of never again being safely able to partake of a substance that pleases me. After a brief period of sadness at the loss of something pleasurable, I would walk out of the doctor's office and not use that drug again. It is a bit like sitting next to an uncle on Thanksgiving Day at the family dinner and offering him cranberries. He might reply; "I like *them,* but *they* don't like me. Please pass the mashed potatoes."

The prospect of avoiding a substance that is injurious to one's health overrides any desire to partake of it, however much it might momentarily please the palate, the feelings, the mind, and the body itself. Yet when applied to the alcoholic and the drug addict, the doctor's advice—"It's the drug that caused it. Stay away from it!"—creates a pain that is deep and worsens with every passing day. It becomes so unbearable that the individual cannot summon up in his mind or imaginings anything else to do to ease the pain but to reach for his drug of choice or some suitable substitute.

I suspect that the reason for this self-destructive and totally irrational reaction is that the person's relationship with the drug is more than physical and mental. The relationship is of a kind that is essential. It is an apparent connection with himself in the very deepest part of him. Without the drug, he feels disconnected with the world around him and with the parts that make him up . . . his feelings, his ideas, his body, even his surroundings. But worst of all, the absence of the drug separates him from who he is, from that part of himself that identifies him as a particular human being with a life of his own.

An alcoholic priest who had known significant success in his ministry told me, "I found that I couldn't sit down long enough and quietly enough to even begin to compose a sermon. The very thought of doing it gave me an incredible urge to have a drink. In fact, every aspect of the ministry became distasteful, and in a strange way almost foreign to me. I was, in a word, extremely agitated and dysfunctional."

Another alcoholic friend confided in me, "I didn't know what was wrong with me. I was so out of touch with what was happening to me that I even feared to see a doctor. I was almost certain that if a doctor did examine me, he would find something unique—something that had never been diagnosed before, something that would make me feel like a freak in this world. Yet, and at the same time, I felt instinctively that there was nothing wrong in the midst of everything being wrong with my life."

No, this disease, though directly related to the physical, is not physical in its essence.

Nor is it in essence a mental disease. Show me an alcoholic or a drug addict, and I know that I am dealing with a person whose mind is very active and whose thought processes are extremely rational. In my experience, a characteristic of an addicted person is that of a thinker. Addicted people can't unplug. If only for a short time they could put their heads in the deep freeze to get some respite from a brain that won't stop thinking!

But to no avail. Alcoholics and drug addicts are endowed with a mental life that is rich and above average. They lie with the best of truths. Their minds operate very well. That is why it is advisable never to get on the level of rationalization or argument with one of these people. You will be guaranteed to be frustrated in your verbal attempt to persuade.

Most addicts have an overactive mind. "To be able *not* to think!" This is the eventual cry of the addicted person.

I am reminded of a story told to me by someone who much later became a drug addict and an alcoholic.

"One day," he said, "in a moment of weariness, I complained to George, my roommate in college, how I wished I could find a way of curtailing my thinking. My friend George asked, 'Oh, is that a problem for you?' I replied, 'Why? Don't you have that problem?' He said, 'No. I only think when I talk!' I couldn't believe my ears, and quickly told him, 'You mean to say that all you have to do is keep your mouth shut and you have peace of mind?' His quiet answer was, 'Yes.' I immediately envied him.

"Only much later in time, after having experienced the full throes of addiction and the relief of recovery, did I come to know that people with less active minds run much less risk of becoming victims of addiction. Not that drugs stopped me from thinking. On the contrary, drugs made my mind race from one thought to another. But the pain was gone. I could think of my family—even of my guilt—painlessly!"

Note well. I am not implying that addicted people are all geniuses. What I am saying is that, intellectually endowed or not, their minds are feverishly functional.

Of course, the disease of addiction plays havoc with the mental capacities of addicts. It makes them think crazy thoughts. It makes them think thoughts that, when really themselves, they would never entertain. It ultimately leads to insanity. It destroys the mind.

A drug addict explained to me how one day, as he was leaving work with his paycheck firmly tucked in his pocket, he thought how crazy it would be if he spent the whole thing on cocaine. Not two minutes later, as he was walking down the street on his way home, did it cross his mind that, although a crazy thought, in his case, since he had paid all of his monthly bills, it would make sense, only for this one week, to spend his whole paycheck on drugs. In fact, with increasing speed, his mind even began to be convinced that he would be crazy not to do it. As a consequence, he wasted his paycheck on cocaine. The next day, when he finally came down from the "high," the first thing that he thought and said to himself was, "I hope that I didn't do that crazy thing and blow my whole pay on drugs!"

Yes, he did! It is interesting to note how from thinking sanely—"It would be insane to spend all this money on drugs"—he falls, in seconds, into total insane thinking—"It would make sense to do it this week." This anecdote underscores my point. Addiction, even prior to drug-taking, makes the mind think in an insane way, but only after it demonstrates a marvelous capacity to operate very sanely.

The insane mind is a consequence of the disease; it is never the cause. The heart of the matter lies elsewhere.

Another theory holds that the addicted person suffers from an emotional imbalance or deficiency. Proponents of this idea state that the feelings of the addict are confused, distorted, and sick.

There is no question that the disease of addiction plays havoc with the emotions of the victims. With the onset of this disease and with its gradual progression, the feelings of the addict are, to say the least, a source of great confusion. They love whom they hate and they hate whom they love. They spend time with strangers and abandon their loved ones. An addicted father cannot stand the presence of his own children, whom he loves deeply.

This was brought home to me when I found myself, one night, visiting the family of an active drug addict. The wife and three children were anxiously awaiting the arrival of the husband and father. When he finally arrived, he retrieved a cold beer from the refrigerator and sat down with us around the kitchen table. At one point in the conversation, he turned to his wife and literally screamed at her, "Get these ———— kids out of here and get them in another room!"

I knew this family for several years. The father loved his children. Yet, in addiction, that intense love became too painful to bear, and literally drove the father to distance himself from his children in a way that was horrifying to them, as you can imagine.

But, again, addiction is not primarily an emotional disease. However much crippled feelings are a consequence of this disease, addicts are gifted at birth with a well-equipped and highly functioning emotive life. No one in the world can boast feelings like the alcoholic and drug addict. These people have deep feelings. Moreover, they experience the whole range of human emotions, and never on a shallow level. They are overactively emotional people. In fact, I believe that a necessary characteristic of an addicted person is that he be at all times very sensitive. Show me a person who doesn't care, and I know that he cannot be addicted. In order to contract this disease, you have to care and to care incessantly.

Families are often witnesses of this phenomenon. Often the most caring member is the one who is most absent "getting high" or "getting drunk." The day my maternal grandmother died, my mother and I were at her bedside. I was eight years old at the time. Upon our return home, we found my father and Uncle Armand (my mother's brother) drunk and still drinking. When my mother told them that Grandma had just died, my father said, "I always said that Armand and I would both be drunk when she died." He didn't say it boastfully. He said it more with a sense of inevitability. There was sadness there, too. I will never forget that scene or my father's words. Neither my father nor my uncle were there at her bedside where they should have been. Yet both loved her very much.

In view of the sensitivity of the addict, it is all the more tragic to consider that addiction eventually destroys the ability to feel in the daily experience of the otherwise very emotive addict.

To sum up, there is, from the beginning, substantially nothing wrong with the bodies, the minds, the feelings, of future addicts. On the contrary, addicts usually are of excellent health, of sound mind, and of rich feeling. Therefore, the source of the problem is elsewhere. Addiction is primarily a spiritual malfunction.

A mystery . . . to be sure!

2
The
Meaning
of
Spiritual

MORE OFTEN THAN NOT, for most people spirituality connotes religion. The saints, Mother Teresa, religious figures of history, nuns, priests, rabbis, ministers—all are considered spiritual. Religious rites and activities are seen as spiritual. Practicing the law of God, fasting, saying prayers, going to church, lighting candles, giving in the collection basket, are thought of as spiritual activities because they are related to religion. In our society, religion and spirituality are linked.

As a result, many alcoholics and addicts feel that the cause of their addiction is somehow related to religion. Either they don't have one, or they become unfaithful in the practice of the one they were given at birth. How many times have I been told by addicted people in recovery, "And would you believe that I once was an altar boy and that I wanted to become a priest!"

Conversely, addicted people without religious training or background find it difficult to accept the disease as a spiritual experience for fear that recovery from it will require an acceptance of and commitment to religion.

But spirituality, and the existence of it, has nothing to do with religion. If it did, the solution to addiction would be found in religion. Alas! Most of the time, it is not found there. In fact, a premature and sick return to religion can plummet a recovering addict right back into his addiction. The guilt, the constant effort, and the too often repeated failures in the attempt to "walk the straight and narrow" become too much to bear, and the addict seeks relief from the pain. This failure all too often becomes proof to the addict that he has in truth slipped from grace into the world of the damned.

I remember in particular one addict who seemingly couldn't be helped. He had a million excuses to delay treatment. Finally, when he couldn't come up with any more reasons for refusing help, he told me in strict confidence that he was different from other addicts in that he knew down deep that he was cursed. He felt he had gone so far in his addiction as well as in the perverse behavior that addiction causes that he was beyond redemption and beyond recovery. He really believed that he was destined to live as an addict and to die an addict.

If spirituality were religion, the avowed and addicted atheist would have no hope of recovery from this disease. By definition, the atheist does not believe in religion as a valid human experience or reality. Yet countless admitted agnostics and atheists have and do experience total recovery. Not only do they stop drinking and using, but they reclaim their rightful connection with life and enjoy real spiritual growth. No, spirituality has nothing to do with religion!

Second, spirituality is not morality. Some people practice the Golden Rule to perfection, and are not one bit spiritual. And you can tell by being in their presence. They don't exude life, enthusiasm, optimism. They are negative, morose, unhappy, bitter, and judgmental of others and of the world. It is possible to be moral and spiritual, but the one does not necessarily assure the existence of the other.

My aunt Blanche, now deceased, is a perfect example of that. Though not addicted to drugs and alcohol, she found her solace in being moral. I hated to visit with her. Her piety and moral standards were so imposing that they made me feel inadequate, guilty, and distrustful of life itself. Her familiar ejaculations still ring in my ear: "What's this world coming to!" "Things seem to be getting worse as we go along!" and, finally, "You better be careful and watch yourself! Otherwise, you're going to turn bad like the rest of them!" Totally unaware, Aunt Blanche for all of her righteousness was a very unhappy person. More than that, she made all of us around her equally unhappy. She was not a giver of life. As a result, she was spiritually off-target.

Being aware, therefore, that spirituality is not religion or morality, what is it? To begin with, I must state that it is impossible to say in words exactly what it is. It is in the domain of mystery. It is like love. Somehow, we can't know what love is. As a result, we can't say in words just precisely what it is. We know what it isn't. Love isn't a kiss. It's more than that. It isn't a hug. It's more than that. It isn't being kind and caring to another. Caring is a result of loving, not love itself. I am kind and I care because I love. Again, to love is more than that.

Therefore, to know and to express the nature of love is impossible.

Yet we do know love. But we can't say what it is, because it isn't on the level of the mind but on a superior level where the mind cannot go. And, therefore, words that express the ideas of the mind are inadequate to express what cannot be known or conceived . . . but rather experienced and lived.

Despite the impossibility of expressing the essence of the nature of the spiritual reality of the human being, I want to attempt to tell you what I am thinking when I speak the words "spiritual" and "spirituality." Spirituality—that part of the human being that is spiritual— is *the thing in him that makes him alive.*

Immediately, I know that I am not talking about my finger. I can cut off my finger and put it at a distance from me. The finger is not me. I am me. It's the same thing with my ideas or my feelings. I am not an idea or a feeling. I am more than that.

The "more than" is the spirit in me . . . that thing that makes me alive, that makes me who I am. Mankind is a mystery. The "thing in me that makes me alive" cannot be conceived or expressed. No doubt there is joy in knowing, but there is ecstasy in not knowing. That explains the ecstasy of seeing a newborn baby where an easy and immediate bond is generated without any prior knowledge of who that little fellow really is.

The less real something is, the more knowable it is. The more real, the less knowable. I can master, for example, the intricacies of the computer and totally be ignorant of why, on a given day, I am angry, fearful, or out of sorts. The reality of my state of being is greater than that of the computer. Similarly, I might well know the content and quantity of the alcohol and cocaine that I am using and be totally oblivious to the alcoholism and drug addiction that plagues me. Again, the disease of addiction is found on a more profound level of reality than the drug itself, which only has a material reality and is found in a flask or a plastic bag. That is also why the child's mind delights in stories of fantasy. Less real than the truth of life, the imaginary world frees the child to know and to exercise a greater degree of control.

The spiritual part of man and woman cannot be expressed in language, not because it is unreal, but because it is so real that no word or expression can capture it or do it justice. The spiritual is another world, another dimension. It is not found in the domain of knowledge but in the domain of experience, of doing, of living.

It is beyond knowledge, and therefore includes it. That is why it is always possible to know life and to know it more and more. Since life is of the spiritual order, we will never know it all. There is, and always will be, more to know. For example, we have that experience in the knowledge of our children and of each other in relationships. At birth, we know only the sex, the looks, and the dimensions of the child. With time, we get to know more of this spiritual being. We experience the vastness of the reality before us in direct proportion to our getting to know . . . to our coming closer to the mystery that helps us touch the infinity of the other. And the excitement of the relationship is increased.

Relationships that flounder and stagnate are those in which the knowledge of the other is stymied and stopped. The mystery of the other person becomes cloudy, and we usually end up saying, "Is that all he or she is?"

And so the spiritual part of man is not his mind or his feelings. It is entirely something else . . . that part of him that makes him alive . . . and alive in the unique way that he is alive.

Nature abhors duplication. Death begets sameness; life begets difference, uniqueness, and individuality. That is why, as we observe the hierarchy of beings, we note a greater difference in the offspring compared with the parents as we ascend the scale of living things. Ants are pretty much indistinguishable, though still different because endowed with life—therefore spiritual. The human species is most remarkable in that the same set of parents gives forth totally different offspring, to the delight of society and of the whole race.

Yes, my spirit is the thing in me that makes me alive and that is nameless—not because it is less real, but because it contains more reality than language can express. It needs another vehicle of expression, of which we will speak further.

And not only is the spirit in me the thing that makes me alive, but it is the thing that makes me alive in the way that I am alive . . . a way that never existed before me and will never repeat itself again. Because of my spirit, I am unique, a gift of gifts that can never exist elsewhere and that is marked with an equally unique destiny.

I believe that it is there, in the spiritual part of me, that addiction—the disease of addiction—has its play. I believe that it is there that it first manifests itself . . . long before the addict encounters the particular drug of his choice. I believe, further, that it is in the spiritual part of the addict that the disease takes root, intensifies, causes the greatest pain, and ultimately spills over or surfaces in the mind, the emotions, and finally the body of the addicted person.

There is no doubt that with time addiction becomes physical, mental, and emotional. But I submit to the reader that addiction is a disease that begins as a spiritual deterioration and, if left unchecked, worsens and gradually invades the mind, the emotions, and eventually the body. By extension, it is capable of destroying everything the addict touches and comes in contact with—his family, his friends, his job, his finances, his reputation, his dignity, his identity, and even his material surroundings.

The wife of an alcoholic and drug addict I knew would periodically call me to complain that her husband had once more come home "high," and had proceeded to take out all of the furniture in order to sell it for the money that he needed to support his habit. One particular night, I received a desperate call from the husband. He was somewhere—God knows where—and was in desperate pain. He cried, shouted, and screamed on the phone. At one point, he told me that he wanted to set fire to his house—all of this in the midst of unintelligible conversation, tears, and pleas for help. No doubt this threat of physical violence was an outward manifestation of an interior pain that could no longer be contained. It was now boiling over and outward toward his material possessions.

My purpose in the following chapters is to describe the effects of this disease on the human spirit and, second, to suggest means one can take in order to restore the spirit to its original health and proper function.

3

The
Beginnings
of Spiritual
Addiction

THERE IS NO QUESTION that to experience life in this world such as it is, such as it always was and always will be, is, I suspect, difficult and at times heartrending. There seems to be no limit to the human capacity to suffer and to endure . . . and to go on. And yet, in the midst of this awful reality, every human person was given a gift. Surely, it is the very gift that we all would want if we didn't have it. This gift can be rarely and even then only minimally experienced in the mind and in the feelings. Its full impact envelops us only when we experience it in the doing, in the living . . . such as an experience of love, of connection with other beings and with life itself. Then it is a kind of ecstasy that words again cannot approximate. Our friends know of it through simple contact with us, and not through wordy communication.

When a person, endowed with this gift, goes into a bar or a shooting gallery and seeks to find happiness—a solution to life—in a chemical, we should know that the use of the chemical itself is not the problem. The chemical is the symptom of the problem in the sense that it alerts us to the existence of the real problem at hand. Too often, when one is emotionally close to the abuser of drugs, the problem appears to be the drug itself. Family members become convinced that if only their alcoholic or drug addict stopped using alcohol and drugs, he or she would be fine.

My mother and I felt just that way about my father. We hoped for the day when he would stop drinking. In our way of thinking, his drinking was the problem. Our lives and his would be all right if only he didn't drink. When he decided to stop drinking, he didn't stop being sick. And we didn't stop being fearful, distrusting, and worried. The booze was gone, but the alcoholism stayed and flourished. My father didn't know one happy day sober in his life.

We made the mistake so many make. We believed that the problem was the alcohol. We know, today, that the problem is somewhere else—that once the drug is removed, the real problem, addiction itself, has to be treated. We know, further, that the problem exists long before the person's first venture to the bar or to the cop man . . . in other words, long before the person's encounter with the drug of his choice.

An addicted person is so immediately taken in by the discovery of a drug because for a long time prior to discovering the drug he has been making superhuman efforts to live a full and successful life. After all, our nature is to live as fully as possible, since life is essentially what defines us. How frustrating it is, for the addicted person, who, since childhood, has been making varied and repeated attempts to make sure he finds his rightful place in life, to discover that he is still down deep disconnected from it.

Countless stories of recovering alcoholics and drug addicts, too numerous to record here, attest to the effort and calculated attempts that went into assuring them a successful life. They got the right education, read the right books, got the right jobs, and entered into the right relationships. They tried to be accommodating to others on the job and in social situations. They were even successful—maybe even reached celebrity status. To no avail. Inside, they remained dissatisfied and painfully out of sync with their own selves. The birth of addiction isn't the result of success or failure in life. It is a state of being that, even in the midst of a host of right moves and good decisions, takes root in the invisible center of a person's life.

You will ask, "But when and how does this phenomenon start?" First of all, let me make clear that neither I nor anyone else knows how or why this disease starts. That is part of the mystery, and another indication to me that addiction is of a spiritual nature in its roots and substance. I feel we will continue to make great strides in deciphering the physical and mental mysteries of this disease in the future. In my opinion and experience, there will be a side to addiction that will forever remain a mystery. For how can man pierce life itself—the individual life and the place where addiction first lifts its head and begins to cause pain?

As to when this process of addiction begins, I feel that it can start at any time. From my experience with addicts, I believe that addiction of whatever kind begins in the early years. I

speak, remember, of the disease as it affects the spirit of the
individual—not the physical being. The question of the
physical origin of this disease—for example, the opinion that
it might be hereditary—belongs to a study other than the one
I am proposing here.

But for anyone who has had this disease, all one has to do
is look back on the early childhood and on the growing-up
years and I believe one will concur . . . the symptoms of the
spiritual pain, of the pain of life, began at that time, persisted
through the years, despite tremendous efforts to deny and
resolve it, and intensified with the passing of time.

This experience holds true of all addicted people, regardless
of their station in life. Rich or poor, majority or minority,
sheltered or deprived, educated or not, all addicts attest to the
fact that, once they recover, they begin to recognize that their
addiction started before the drug, and was similar in nature, if
not always in circumstance, to their counterparts'.

I want to describe to you what this early experience is. If I
had to use one word to say it, I suppose that it would be the
word "alienation." Life is a connection with something, even
if that something is mysterious and not to be known. It is
therefore no surprise that the first manifestations of the disease
of addiction is a kind of disconnection that is deep, persistent,
and progressive. The alienation is embedded in the being of the
person. As a result, it is often not felt or known in its earliest
manifestations. Alienation surfaces in time.

Of course, all human beings experience disconnection,
alienation. The resolution of alienation is precisely found in
experiencing the trauma of being born, of growing up, of being
a teenager, and of finally coming into one's own—of connecting, in a word, with oneself. Alienation is certainly experienced
by all people—both addicted and nonaddicted. However,

there is a difference in the case of the addicted person—a difference that I intend to return to and explain at the end of this chapter.

In order to describe in clearer terms the experience of alienation in the addicted person before he discovers the addiction of his choice, I want to mention different forms that this alienation takes in the early life of the addict.

THE FEELING OF
BEING DIFFERENT

The addict feels different. Or he is afraid that he will discover that he is different. This is a vague feeling. It is even more than a feeling. It is a state of being that, so the addict thinks to himself, he will with luck and care resolve in time.

A fortyish recovering alcoholic and drug addict started drinking and using drugs when he was twenty-five. He stated that, as a teenager, he was strikingly handsome. He also exercised with weights, and had developed a well-muscled body. Yet when he was with his friends, his good looks and physical fitness were of little consolation to him. In his mind, the other boys—some of whom were also good-looking and well-built—seemed always to have the edge on him. Not that he denied his own appearance, but somehow there was, in his case, an element missing that made him feel inadequate, disconnected, always a bit beneath the desired norm.

Today, that addict, as he showed me pictures of himself as a teenager, laughs at the unfounded concern that needlessly increased his discontent and discomfort.

This experience is vague in the addicted person and not that threatening. It's akin to feeling the early mist before the coming of the rain.

NEGATIVITY

When the chances of a good result are fifty-fifty, the future addict even in childhood is instinctively prone to dread the worst. "I remembered my aunts," declared a recovering addict, "the night before the Fourth of July, making sandwiches for the family picnic, all the while talking grown-up talk. I would pick up on their conversation and hear them say how they hoped that it 'doesn't rain tomorrow.' And I would go to bed more afraid that it would rain than confident that it would be a sunny day."

This tendency to embrace the negative more readily is an inbred instinct in the future addict. He or she is at a very young age sensitive to what the family doesn't have: a car, a house, a computer, etc. The very thought of planning for a future activity is riddled at the outset with the pain that the plans will be ruined. The pre-addict finds it difficult to see the bright side or to appreciate what he has, because the connection with what he doesn't have is so insistent and controlling. The negative point of view takes center stage at the expense of the positive outlook, which becomes faint and easily overlooked.

In the twelve-step programs, members explain it this way: A person can consider half a glass of water as half-empty or half-full. Prior to the discovery of the drug, the future addict automatically sees it as half-empty.

COMPARING

A recovering addict readily admits, "As a child, I was convinced that other families were better than mine. I knew that on a Sunday afternoon, everybody was on their way to somewhere, doing something interesting. Every family, that is, except mine. Everybody had to worry less than I, because obviously they were more together. Never did I stop to ask myself why. The reason was unquestionable. It was a given."

This instinct to compare with others and inevitably come up short has nothing to do with deprivation, being up against it, or just plain out of luck. Even in prosperous circumstances in which the individual is blessed with a normal family life, a proper education, and a good job, the need to compare and to feel cheated somehow gnaws at him and seems impossible to overcome.

A recovering drug-addict friend of mine recalls that he was reared in a well-to-do and loving family with a younger sister and a twin brother. He admits being jealous of the sister, feeling that she received more attention from his parents. Pursuing a career in graphic art for which he was well suited, he abruptly abandoned this course without giving a reason.

In recovery, it came to light that he dropped his pursuit of graphic art because his brother was successful in the same field. In the process of comparing himself with his brother, this man elected to put himself in second place and sacrificed the very line of work in which he excelled. Today, thanks to the healing he found in recovery, he is employed as a successful graphic designer.

SOCIAL AWKWARDNESS

Another addict remembers that when he was photographed by a family member, he felt uncomfortable from the first mention of it to the final click of the camera. He would invariably take on a body posture that was not natural, but self-conscious—not to enhance himself, but to qualify as the human being that he was supposed to be. For the addict, to be only as I am is to fall short.

Yet the pre-addict is very socially conscious. He is keenly aware that he is made to connect with people around him. As a result, he suffers the pain of hell when he finds himself in a gathering of people who are all interacting while he is alone not talking to anyone. He has the instinct that like everybody else, he should be engaged in lively conversation with someone.

More than that, the future addict harbors in his heart the deep desire to be the center of attention. He seeks recognition and praise. I think it is his deep-seated sense of alienation that triggers constant uncertainty of himself and makes him so needy of repeated affirmation in the form of recognition from his peers.

The future addict receives praise with awkwardness and inappropriate protestations. If he is asked to perform—for example, play the piano or sing a song—he steadfastly refuses, breaks into tears, or runs out of the room. No doubt he craves the opportunity to gain attention. But more powerful yet is his fear of being judged inadequate—of being labeled incompetent and ultimately a failure.

He has a prophetic sense that the unknown part of his being that is not right will become visible for all to see. Hence his awkwardness and, later, his regret at having missed the secretly sought-after opportunity to be recognized.

GENERAL FEELING OF DISSATISFACTION

Another symptom of the spiritual disease of addiction is a general feeling of having been left out, of being bored. The child addict wonders why on earth he was born. What is his place in life? What is meant for him to do? Left alone, he is lost and dreams of a person, an event, a happening, that might fill the void. The idea of creativity, of inner resources, escapes him completely. If the thought comes of using his imagination to fill the gap, he quickly dismisses that possibility as inept, unsure, and doomed to fail.

Many times, if not always, these traits, which have their source in a deep feeling of alienation, of disconnection with the reality of oneself and of one's surroundings, are not conscious, sometimes not even felt. But they are always there, deep in what I call the spiritual being of the individual. Later, and progressively, these experiences are felt and forever analyzed.

As this deep dissatisfaction surfaces in the emotive and conscious life of the person, he or she sets out to find ways to resolve the discomfort that ensues. The future addict tries with a superhuman effort that is constant and relentless to resolve the alienation and feel at home in the world and within himself. The following modes of behavior are the immediate responses of the future addict to unpleasant situations.

AVOIDANCE
AND ESCAPE

A recovering alcoholic recalls, "At some of our Boy Scout meetings, I was terrified at the prospect of taking part in what then was called knot-tying contests. Two lines of scouts formed the two teams. As one got to the head of the line, a scout leader would call at random a certain type of knot that the scout at the head of the line had to tie as fast as he could. The first line of scouts to finish was declared the winner. The impossibility for me to connect with the hope of winning filled me with the fear of almost certain failure, especially when it would be my turn to tie the knot requested by the leader. As a result, I would develop, when that activity was announced, real or imagined stomach cramps so that I had to be excused, or I would seek out the assistant scoutmaster to volunteer my services in other areas in order to escape participation in the contest. I would even try to guess at which scout meetings these contests would be held and avoided attending those meetings altogether."

Escape from a reality that brings to the surface the profound discomfort of the addictive person it as dangerous and destructive as it is effective. This escape gets the individual off the hook, but it ushers him into the land of fantasy. It furthers the belief that one can control life—that to escape a situation is an infallible way of eliminating it. The more escape is practiced, the more one believes that it works.

Escape takes on many forms. Recovering addicts have reported that they escape unpleasant realities such as family situations, involvement in group activities, loneliness, and even despair by immersing themselves in books, television, piano lessons, masturbation, model airplanes, and stamp collecting—anything to avoid dealing with the harsh reality of the moment.

Even at a young age, some find their escape in religion, where they feel unthreatened and comfortable in the knowledge that people will be nice and charitable to them and not put them on the spot. It is called hiding from life in church.

ISOLATION

Children who are afflicted with the spiritual disease of addiction love and thrive on human company. They are social by nature, more so than the average child. Yet these children, because of their inner discomfort and inability to connect with themselves, always wonder if they will do the right thing—the normal thing others would do. Full of certain fear that they won't, they seek refuge in being alone. "Rather be alone—which I hate—than be in company and fail" is a common experience of the child addict.

Sarah would isolate herself in her room, where she had nothing to do. Basically, she would read and reread the entry she made in her diary the day before, arrange and rearrange the items on her dresser and night table. Most of the time, she would find herself looking out the window and seeing only the reruns of her fantasies and dreams.

It isn't that Sarah found happiness in her room. In reality, she hated it, and her parents often complained about all the time she spent there—alone with nothing to do. In her heart,

Sarah agreed with them, but somehow the certainty that being alone gave was better than the uncertainty of being with the rest of the family in the common rooms. In the latter, she never knew how or when she would be spoken to and maybe put on the spot. Alone in her own room, she was in control, however much loneliness and inactivity there were painful.

ACT AS IF

Haven't we all had this experience as a child? We are exposed to it all of our lives. Someone asks us how we are, and we say, "Fine!" when we aren't fine at all. So, too, the future addict uses this ploy as a remedy, an escape from the constant discomfort that is there. Notice I didn't say discomfort that one *feels,* because even when the addict is not conscious of his alienation, it is at work in him, making the art of living a chore. The addict believes he would be better if he were smart enough and alert enough to observe how the rest of the seemingly successful human race managed to do it.

As a result, the pre-addict lacks self-confidence. He doesn't trust his feelings. He's convinced that his gut reactions to people and events are flawed. They are selfish or uninformed. They are hasty or wrong. They, somehow, lack truth.

For that reason, he doesn't say anything or react according to his instincts, to his own truth. He denies his feelings and stuffs them. To give in to an act of his own terrifies him.

Betraying his own instincts and reactions, the pre-addict searches for the correct response. He attempts to glean the correct behavior from his observation of others. Unconsciously and with time, he becomes an expert. He learns the art of people-pleasing at his own expense.

This posture has the advantage of making him momentarily acceptable, but his disloyalty to his real self results in disaster. It serves to deepen his alienation—that gap between what is acceptable and who he is. He in fact puts himself in the lie that separates him more and more from himself.

ANALYZE, RATIONALIZE, AND JUDGE

Of course, if a person feels that he has less and less control over his environment, his situation in life, the intelligent conclusion is to exercise that control in the only area left. And that is to exercise *mental* control and power, which gives at least the intellectual satisfaction of being in charge of one's world. It assuages the feeling of alienation by establishing a connection with people, places, and things—albeit untrue in the real world, but at least true in the world of the mind.

If someone that I admire snubs me, it is easier for me to dismiss that person than to admit being hurt. Similarly, if I don't see the possibility of being rich, it is easier for me to condemn people with money than to reveal the pain of not being rich.

This behavior prompts the future addict to rationalize the unpleasant real in order to arrive at a judgment favorable to himself. It protects the addict from blame. It justifies him, and it condemns the other. It is a form of control and power when no other means of control is possible. Failing a test in school, he judges the questions unfair rather than admit his own inability to answer them. Being turned down for a job, he puts the blame on the bias and abrasiveness of the person who conducted the interview rather than on his own lack of qualifications for the job. From then on, anything unpleasant that the pre-addict can't control and ward off through other means is meticulously analyzed—that is to the condemnation of the person, place, or thing at hand.

A recovering addict describes this phenomenon from his childhood: "I had an uncle Bill. Every time he visited, he would tease me until I cried. I tried everything to regain comfort. I would hide in the closet; I begged my parents to not allow him in the house. They merely laughed at me and made me feel more inadequate than I already felt. As a last resort, I decided in my mind that he was the worst man alive, that I would hate him all my life, and that I wouldn't bother with him as soon as I was old enough to make my own decisions. Furthermore, I wouldn't acknowledge even his death, and I wouldn't attend his funeral."

One sees in this early resorting to rationalization and mind control the seeds of the full-blown disease, which is often referred to as a disease of rationalization, constant analysis, and harsh judgment. Reality becomes stranger and more distant. It nudges the pre-addict into further fantasy, and alienates him from real people, places, and things.

SHYNESS/BRAVADO

This is another manifestation of alienation in the young, and in particular in the young and future addict. In a situation where attention is focused on the individual, a person resorts to acting in a very timid way with the feeling of wanting to disappear into the wall of a given room. Or he fights the malaise by resorting to what I call bravado or "cockiness." In either case, the outward behavior isn't at all a reflection of the real person.

APPROVAL-SEEKING

For lack of any inner self-justification, the young addict constantly seeks approval from the outside. For that reason, he needs to excel in something, and revels in the praise that results. It isn't rare in the history of addicts to find a model child.

Rudy, a now-recovering alcoholic, told me this story, which happened when he was a child, long before he became an active drinker.

"We were a large family. My mother had thirteen siblings. One of her brothers had a grocery store. The nephews and nieces loved to help in the store. Of course, all of them would clandestinely take a piece of penny candy from the candy counter.

"I never did. Oh, I wanted to desperately! But I preferred the approval of the adult family members when they would call me the best worker of all the cousins because I didn't, like them, take candy from the counter. I, they said, could be trusted.

"The approval was my reward, and at that time preferable to having the candy. Today, I must add, I think that I would prefer the candy over the approval."

PROJECTION

Who hasn't imagined better times once he has grown and joined the adult world? The young addicted person constantly uses this means as a source of hope. A recovering addict told me,"When I was in grammar school, I became convinced that there was nothing I could do about my miserable life at the present time. I was, however, equally convinced that once out of grammar school and in high school, my life would change. No more would I feel alienated, incomplete, inadequate. And then came high school. Things seemed for the first month or two to be better. But in quick order the same uncomfortability returned, and with it the sure hope that, once in college, for sure it would be resolved. But again, in college it wasn't. Basically, the same problems of alienation, of disconnection, resurfaced, and somehow were more intense and caused more pain. Then I entertained the hope that once in my career, once established in 'adult life,' the old problem of being uncomfortable in life would disappear. And again, the adult life came but the alienation worsened."

Later on, in recovery, this budding addict will learn the difference between planning one's life and projection. To plan is to foresee a series of steps to take that are most apt to lead to a specific goal. Projection also means taking certain steps, but to the addict these steps almost magically insure certain desired results.

In the addict's way of thinking, to take the steps or the action *is* to assure the result. Again, the disease, even before the use of the drug, puts the addict in a very unrealistic frame of reality. It sets up an expectation that doesn't always follow. For example, if I set out to make money in order to be happy, I might well succeed in making money but still find myself unhappy. If I want to get to Chicago, I might take the train destined for Chicago but, because of an accident, never get there. The pre-addict approaches life with this erroneous equation. He equates the means with the end. Much later in recovery, he will be encouraged to alter his view of things. He will be advised to take the best means at hand and surrender to the results over which he has no control.

PERFECTIONISM

It is no wonder that the young addict either does nothing or does it to perfection. This trait of perfectionism, as like all the other traits mentioned above, is a hallmark of addiction from its inception throughout its progression. In fact, at the end of its progression, most addicts practically do nothing at all. They don't even attempt to do anything, knowing that they are incapable of making it perfect.

In this respect, I will never forget one of my own alcoholic father's favorite slogans. He would repeat it over and over again: "If you can't do it right, don't do it at all."

Strangely enough, this trait of perfectionism can also work the other way. Many future addicts are very active and become workaholics. It seems as if they keep working in the hope that they will succeed in getting it all done once and for all.

A Texan I once knew, who became a raging alcoholic in his later years, separated himself from his family at sixteen years of age. After bouncing around different parts of the country, including a stint in Canada, he finally settled in New York City. He quickly got a job at one of the Howard Johnsons in Manhattan. Looking back, he readily admits to "working my little buns off. In fact, I would sometimes work double and even triple shifts. And this job was hectic. Right in midtown Manhattan, the place was always jumping both day and night. Yet whenever one of the waiters wanted someone to replace him on his shift, he always came to me, and I was only too glad to oblige."

This need never to say no to his employer and co-workers was, in fact, a denial of his many needs as a human being—his need to rest, to play, and, plainly, to live. As in so many other cases, perfectionism in the addictive personality is a facet of alienation from self. It doesn't allow for one's humanity with all of its limitations and possibilities.

These ingredients form the makeup of the alienation experienced by the future addict. These early symptoms of the spiritual disease of addiction and the unsuccessful attempts to resolve this alienation cause the young addict pain—consciously or unconsciously—that destroys energy and strength.

At first sight, the scenario I have described doesn't appear different from the experience of every child in his infancy, early childhood, and teenage years. Yet there are two major differences.

It is clear that all children experience alienation. They go through a period of awkwardness and of what we call "growing pains." In time, as the child grows and comes into his own, he grows *out* of the initial alienation that as humans we all undergo. The young and future addict, on the other hand, doesn't grow *out* of it . . . he grows *into* it. In other words, the addicted person doesn't find an accommodation with the fear, the isolation, the negativity, the dissatisfaction, the social awkwardness, the feeling of being different. On the contrary, all of these characteristics grow with him, so that when he reaches the ages of twenty, thirty, fifty, and even seventy, all of these experiences become more intense and more crippling. They grow with the individual and become a part of his nature with the passage of time, the kind of life that he *is*. And the anomaly is established. The "nonlife" experiences of alienation and disconnection, the "nonlife" solutions for resolving alienation and disconnection, become the very life of this individual.

A cruel situation to be in! A baffling problem that is easier to deny than to face is created.

Though the average child experiences this alienation, sometimes physically, often mentally and emotionally, the future addicted child experiences it profoundly in his spirit—in the spiritual part of him—in that part of him that gives him life, that makes him alive. In a word, although deep in all of us, this alienation that we all experience and work through invades the deepest part of the addict's being. It buries itself so deep that by the time it surfaces, the individual is already very sick, incapable of self-diagnosis, and, in his eyes at least, incapable of recovery.

The beginnings of addiction are subtle but very real. They are lodged in the part of us that is the most real—the very core of our beings. It is said that addiction is an inside job. And well it is. By the time it becomes full-blown and visible in the behavior and physical habits of the person addicted, its damage to the spirit is extensive and requires much time and effort to restore.

Before we speak of the spiritual recovery of addiction, let us consider the progression of this disease. What happens when the person addicted for a long time in the spirit finds the drug of his choice? Although this book focuses on alcohol and drugs, addiction also can be found in reference to food, work, money, sex, rage, religion, and people, as well as countless other addictions as yet undiscovered.

As we now begin to investigate the consequences of the discovery of a chemical substance by a person already sick in his spirit, I want to stress that, from addiction's inception, the person afflicted is in pain. It is a pain that even he cannot identify and name . . . a pain that is spiritual, and which, as it grows and progresses, will in time become mental, emotional, and physical.

4
The Discovery of the Drug

BY THIS TIME, the addicted person is in great pain. It is a pain that he doesn't share with anyone, because he is convinced already that nobody ever experienced life in quite the way he does. As far as the addict is concerned, the people he comes in contact with, whom he observes on the streets, in the supermarkets, in his home, all seem to have found the key that he thinks we all must find in order for life to work.

Little does he realize that life, once given, works by itself . . . except when someone decides to take matters into his own hands and becomes convinced that finding a magic formula will solve life's problems.

Our addict is now an adult . . . in some cases a young adult in his teens, in other cases in his twenties, thirties, forties, fifties, right on through the eighties and nineties. This spiritual disease knows no race and no age. It can appear anywhere, anytime, and in anybody.

From an imperceptible, invisible, at times unconscious, beginning in the spirit of the person, the disease gradually progresses by surfacing to the emotions and the mind. At whatever the age this occurs, the addictive individual now is more and more alienated from his feelings. There are some feelings he doesn't like and doesn't think he should have. He has the same experience with the ideas that cross his mind. In his way of looking at things, some thoughts are justifiable and others are not. In the latter case, he believes he should simply not have them.

A recovering alcoholic priest, who served as the academic dean of an excellent prep school in the Northeast, shared this intimate experience with me:

"Once a month my mother and father would come to the prep school to visit me. I loved them dearly, but these visits were very painful to me. When I would hear them arguing and bickering, when I would see them sick or unhappy about something, I would panic inside and feel so helpless. In a word, I felt so emotionally close that I could never enjoy their company with the ease that I always wanted to have. The thought would sometimes cross my mind as I watched them drive off in the distance that I wished that they would have a car accident on the way back home and that both would die instantly. In that case, there would be a double funeral, and I would be finished with the whole business once and for all. In my sick mind, I felt that in their deaths, I would be relieved of the pain.

"Needless to say, such thoughts and feelings only increased my guilt and my low self-esteem. How could someone think like that and be a good son? I felt utterly defeated within myself. Somehow, as I look back, I never shared this uncomfortable state of soul with anyone."

No, the addict never shares this strangeness with anyone. A mistake . . . but an understandable mistake when you consider that the addict, as much as he would like to unburden himself, decides to retreat into an ever-increasing and destructive silence. He has to, since there is no word to express the pain that he feels. The addict is, by instinct, keenly aware on the level of experience that his pain is inexpressible.

If a friend were to ask him this question: "What's wrong?" he couldn't answer except to say, "I don't know." For a lot of us, and especially for the addict, not to know, not to be able to express something in human words, is tantamount to being out of control, to being odd, which invites the sneer, the judgment, the condemnation . . . the alienation of the rest of the human race and ultimately the condemnation of oneself.

So the addict doesn't share his pain. As a result, the pain intensifies. By now, he is a walking time bomb—going through the motions of living, but really unliving, disconnected from the very situations and people with whom he is interacting. It's a little like being dead while alive. The worst of the worst.

Through varied circumstances, our friend finds the drug of his choice. Finally, he's getting somewhere! I knew an alcoholic who didn't drink until later in life for the simple reason that he was brought up in an alcoholic family. Convinced that booze was an evil thing, he always avoided it. The day he found the drink, he said to me, "That's why people drink!" What he meant is that with all the undesirable results of alcoholic drinking in his family, he couldn't fathom for the life of him why people, witnessing these ill-effects, would drink. Being an alcoholic and discovering the drink, he instantly knew the reason why people drank. Little did he realize that to all nonalcoholics, his newly discovered reason for drinking didn't apply.

With the ingestion of the first drink, the addicted person is immediately filled with well-being ... a well-being that he knew in his heart he had to find in order to live effectively. He is filled with hope. From now on, it's going to be Christmas for him, too. He is going to be able to live like everybody else.

Instantly, life, so constantly difficult for him in the past, now seems manageable. First of all, he immediately experiences that he can relax and party with the drug. He can now enjoy himself like never before. Family problems don't seem as threatening as they did before. Problems on the worksite, with the boss, are resolved instantly ... in intention at least. The drug addict under the influence of the drug has no trouble deciding, "Tomorrow I'll speak to the boss and clear this up for good!" Problems, if any, with one's culture, one's origins, one's race, become less difficult to live with. Sex becomes easier to talk about, to anticipate, and to perform. Even God, for those who are bothered by matters of faith and of supreme power, seems less problematic. The Supreme Being becomes easier to know and control or easier to discard and ignore. In a word, life becomes what the addict always sought to make it—a pleasurable experience with all problems solved. He becomes, for the first time, a friend of life. And for the first time, life is also on *his* side.

RESULTS ON THE HUMAN SPIRIT

This description of what the addict experiences when he finally discovers the drug of his choice conveys the immediate and general effects of the drug. But what of the results of the discovery on the human spirit?

According to my observations, there are five main results I would like to discuss.

ALIENATION BEGINS TO DISSOLVE

First and most important, the interior pain of alienation begins to lessen. The addict's basic disconnection, which accompanied all of his thoughts, his feelings, and his relationships with other people and with the world in which he lives, seems to melt away.

No more does he suffer that basic difference that put him outside the mainstream and that was more than a mere feeling. Rather, it is a state of being that seems lodged in the deepest part of his nature, beyond the mind and the emotions. Always lurking there, it raises its head in good times and bad times—in times of "feeling good" and of "feeling bad."

With the help of the drug, he feels a brotherhood with all people—a feeling that he longed to have all of his life. No longer does he compare with others. For the first time, he feels superior to all people. I'm the best in the world, he thinks, Come join with me. His "high" makes it impossible for him to accept that others might not be able to enjoy life. Now, he knows how to live. So he can't imagine that anyone would not want to be in his company. He's so much fun and he's such a good guy. He's found the art of living.

No longer does he have to live in negativity. In fact, now, there is no such thing as negativity. Who cares if it's raining or if there's a nuclear attack down the street? No longer is there any need of fear. In fact, fear disappears entirely. What a relief! Especially for the addicted person, who, for as long as he remembers, feared when there was no need to fear. Now, he has no fear even when fear is normal and healthy.

As a result, the alcoholic challenges the biggest brute in the bar. Despite protestations from his drinking companions, he insists on beating up someone who evidently has already won the fight. The drug addict, despite debts and a possible contract on his life, ventures out in dangerous territory because he has to cop more drugs for his next "high."

For several years, there was in my neighborhood an old man who was an invalid and got around in a wheelchair. He was alcoholic, and apparently lived in the streets. Rather quiet, he never bothered anybody. On certain evenings, returning from work, I would be aghast to see him, wheelchair and all, in the middle of the busy thoroughfare, directing traffic. At any given moment, he could have got hit by the fast and numerous oncoming automobiles. Although I was at times so afraid for him that I couldn't bear to watch, he was having the time of his life, experiencing not the shadow of fear.

Fearless, the addicted person is also no longer socially awkward. On the contrary, he seeks the limelight and the center of attention. Even when not asked, he insists on performing and entertaining what he perceives to be a fawning and begging public.

While the addicted person was always dissatisfied, even in the midst of a positive human situation and experience, now he is totally satisfied even in the worst of situations. Anything is a reason for buying a round of drinks or for throwing a party. The reason could be a birthday, an anniversary, or even a funeral. The guideline now is "Don't let clouds get in the way. Brush them aside and have fun—enjoy life. After all, that's what we are here for."

Not only are the strains of alienation eliminated in the

discovery of the drug of choice, but all the futile attempts on the part of the addict to cover up, to resolve the deep-down feeling that was the hallmark of his very being, become unnecessary.

No more does the addict feel the need to resort to the trick of escape and avoidance when he finds himself uncomfortable in a situation. Now, the addict, instead of avoiding situations, provokes them. The alcoholic, once inebriated, will sometimes go to any lengths to get himself arrested by a policeman who happens by. If the officer doesn't respond, it is all too frequent an occurrence for the alcoholic to go up to him and dare him to arrest him.

At this stage of development of the disease, the addicted person will go out of his way to seek out the person whom he would avoid at all cost when sober. He makes long-distance telephone calls to people in his past and carries on a maudlin conversation. Or he becomes irate and offensive, to the confusion and shock of the listener at the other end of the line.

Isolation is another unnecessary ploy used by the addict before he finds the drug that resolves his alienation. With physical addiction, isolation has no more meaning once the addict has found his drug of choice. The addict doesn't need to isolate. He feels perfectly comfortable in all situations. Even alone, the addict is never alone again. He lives in a world populated by millions of people, even if he is alone in his living room staring at the television or on the street corner enjoying a heroin nod.

The drug itself becomes *the* connection, and makes all other connections with people, places, events, or things totally unmeaningful and inconsequential. The drug addict doesn't suffer from being disconnected, and has no need to distance himself from people. The drug—which is outside of him—

gives him the illusion of a spiritual connection—which he doesn't experience without the drug.

In the beginning, the drug makes all connections with others easy, natural, and desirable. So the drug addict looks for opportunities to party, for people to get high with. With the inevitable progression of the disease, that is, with the ever-growing connection with the drug, a sense of greater well-being and growing satisfaction develops; no other connections are sought. The drug addict's sphere of movement and of activity gradually shrinks to the immediate corner where he "hangs out," to the fewer and fewer people with whom he "hangs out," and ultimately to nobody else except the "cop man" he increasingly needs.

For the alcoholic, the same phenomenon takes place. At first, the drunk seeks the company of other people, revels in barhopping, seeks out drinking parties, and spends hours in the social setting of his home bar (his watering hole of choice) in dancing, card-playing, pool-playing, or idle and lengthy chatter with whoever will listen. In progression, the alcoholic is less and less invited to parties, nor does he seek them out as before. By giving him the illusion of being in the company of multitudes and in the center of life's feverish activity, the alcohol makes social interaction with real people obsolete. His friends change and then disappear. His drinking rounds become limited ultimately to one bar, and finally to none at all. He ends up drinking at home or buying a bottle that he nurses at a nearby park or on an unsavory and isolated stoop.

The process is fascinating. From seeking out isolation to avoid connections that don't work and cause pain, the addicted person makes a connection with a drug that takes him out of his isolation by making other connections painless, to immerse him finally in an isolation so terrible that only more of the drug and only the drug can conceal and remedy.

The drug, while restoring his connections, strips the addict of his human need and real desire to connect. In fact, as the disease progresses, the addict will seek out isolation as the best circumstance in which he can enjoy his high.

The addict no longer has to act "as if." Now, the addict acts out. As soon as an idea hits his brain, he doesn't conceal it by acting "as if," but rather puts the idea into action. That is why there are sudden shifts from camaraderie to violence in bars and at parties.

Al, a gentle and tolerant man by nature, wasn't particularly drawn to members of the cloth in general or to me in particular. Yet whenever we would meet, he always treated me with respect and proper deference. One early evening, I literally bumped into him on the street. I instantly noticed that he was drunk. Regaining his balance from our unintended collision, he began to rail against me and even threaten to hit me. In a sober state, Al would have pleasantly greeted me and engaged in surface but civilized conversation. The alcohol caused him to "act out," that is, to simultaneously recognize me and take hostile action against me. The next time I saw him, he was sober, and awkwardly apologized for his unwarranted behavior.

The addict used to rationalize and judge in order to preserve some kind of semblance of control over his environment. No more! The addict at this stage doesn't think. The normal thought process is replaced by impressions, impulses, isolated ideas that pop into the mind of the drugged person and that are unrelated and disconnected from any other thought that may precede or follow. The alcoholic or drug addict who is high does not think coherently. He should say to himself, for example, "That policeman is annoyed by my boisterous behavior. I better cool it or I just might get arrested." His thinking pattern is more akin to "Why is that policeman standing there? He's a jerk." Little wonder that the scene ends in his arrest, which the addict feels is unfair and irrelevant.

The drug that is the main switch for all of his connections eliminates the addict's need to rationalize or to analyze a situation. The thought process is replaced by the drug, which produces instant and disconnected ideas that in turn lead the addict into irrational situations. This helps to explain why the professional community views addiction as a form of insanity caused by the gradual deterioration of the brain.

Working in a rehabilitation facility a few years ago, I met a woman in her sixties, who, although admitted as a patient suffering from alcoholism, denied that she had a problem. A charming person, she declared that her son was a good and loving boy, but had the erroneous impression that she drank too much.

She expressed all of this with such calm and kindness toward her son that I began to think that maybe she was right and the son was indeed reading his mother's situation incorrectly. It was only when I finally met with the son and expressed my concern to him that he pulled out pictures of his mother's house, including shots of her bedroom. The sight was incredible. Her bedroom was a shambles, with the floor covered with empty beer cans and bottles.

When I told the mother that I had spoken to her son and that he had showed me pictures of her bedroom, she merely smiled and——oblivious to the evidence that I myself had seen——told me that I was mistaken and had been "had" by the tales of her well-meaning but misdirected son. This woman's ability to think rationally had already been seriously impaired.

In the past, the addict used projection to maintain a modicum of comfort. If things were wrong now, maybe later things would get better. With the discovery of the drug, projection makes no sense. The future, as well as the past, becomes the present.

The future is now. That is why the addict is free of problems. If tomorrow he has to face an unpleasant situation, all he has to do is indulge in his drug of choice. Instantly, the problem seems easy to deal with and to resolve. This is so true that the addict gives it no more thought . . . as if, for having thought about it, it were just as good as dealt with . . . until the next morning, when he realizes that the situation is the same—untouched, unresolved, and more frightening than before.

The past also becomes the present. That is why the drunk and the addict dwell on the past. They like to speak about it, constantly mull over it, and even become teary-eyed at the slightest consideration of it.

An alcoholic/addict I once knew at a time when he was at the worst point of his addiction would unfailingly overwhelm me with his unending talk and ramblings about his brother—a brother whom he dearly loved and grew up with, but hadn't spoken to for the last ten years. You couldn't get this man to say a good word about his brother when sober. He said that he hated him and would do so for the rest of his life. But, when the man was drunk or high, the brother of his past would come to life again, and the addict would go on for hours (if I was patient enough to hear him out) about the "good times" they had had together when they were children.

One night, and against my protestations, he even called up

his brother long distance, and insisted that I speak to him on the phone. Since we had never met one another, this was embarrassing for both of us . . . and no less so, I suspect, for my addict friend when he later received his telephone bill and couldn't even remember having placed the call.

The point is that while he was "high," the past experience of his brother became a real experience of the present.

Many times the addict, now in recovery, looks back at the discovery of his drug of choice with gratitude that he found it when he did. His pain prior to the drug was so intense and of such a long duration with no relief at all that he wonders what would have happened to him if he hadn't found the relief he did in the drug. In retrospect, the drug is a boon—a relief that hastens him on to greater pain, but also to the authentic and genuine resolution that only recovery can give the addict.

For now, the first effect of discovering the drug is a new-found comfort that dissolves that nasty feeling of alienation.

POSSIBILITY OF CONTROLLING LIFE

The second effect of the initial use of the drug is the realization that there is a possibility of controlling life (including God). This realization emerges at a time when the addict begins to panic. For some strange reason, all addicted people, before they find the drug of their choice, grow up with the idea that life for a person is successful only if one finds that magical thing, that key, that mysterious something that makes life work. As they look at the people around them and become certain that these individuals have found the magic wand, the art of living, they ask themselves, "What is this mysterious key?"

The addict imagines that it is all kinds of things. For example, maybe the key is making sure that one avoids having enemies, that one gets along with all people. Maybe it's being aggressive and speaking out. Or it might be true that the more noise one makes, the more one wins and gets his way. The list of imaginings here is unending, and God knows the addict is willing to put all of the items to the test.

Now, the addict is saved from panic, and again just in the nick of time, by the skin of his teeth . . . convinced again that his superhuman efforts to save face, not to deteriorate into the strange human he feels convinced he is—in a word, to not be the only failure at living—have prevailed. The drug opens up to him the possibility of living successfully as he thinks all human beings live.

Before he began to use drugs, Ramon lived with his wife and two children aged five and three in New York City. The family was on welfare and lived in a run-down neighborhood, and life was not happy. His relationship with his wife was strained, and he was beginning to abuse his children physically. Ramon himself was unconsciously bored, lonely, and depressed. In his mind, a job, if he could find one, would give him a renewed purpose, self-esteem, and a hope of bettering his family's living conditions. He was certain that the job was the "key" that would finally open up his life to the realization of all his dreams.

Suddenly, he had a job, and for a while Ramon felt centered. He was proud of himself again. He had found the answer, and nothing, so it seemed to him, could go wrong. He had even put together a down payment for a secondhand car. But the feeling of discontent, the burden of daily living, slowly returned. Once again, things seemed to be getting out of control. He couldn't seem to hang on to life once he thought he had it in the palm of his hand.

At this point, he was introduced to drugs. Co-workers enticed him to try some crack. Within six months, this devastating drug started him on the road of truly believing, once again, that he was in charge of his destiny.

Overnight, Ramon abandoned his car at JFK Airport without telling anyone, not even his family or his employer, flew to a remote village in Puerto Rico, and lived with his mother. Sure that in a radical change of place and lifestyle he would rediscover the happy life, within a month of his move he contacted his wife, instructed her to pack their belongings, prepare the two boys, and move down to the island with him. The hesitancy in her voice at the prospect of making such a radical move prompted Ramon to convince her at length of how things down there would be great for all of them. Finally, she went.

What awaited Ramon's family in Puerto Rico can only be described as a sheer disaster. By this time, Ramon was heavily into drugs and debt. He was jobless, and his mother had evicted him from her house. At last word, the wife and children were staying with Ramon's mother while looking for the necessary money to return to New York City. As for Ramon, they hadn't seen him recently, and even feared for his life.

From Ramon's long search for a solution to life—before the use of drugs—he had reached the point of once again believing in the possibility of fixing his life through the proper maneuver of external circumstances and situations—this time under the influence of the drug or, if you will, of the full-blown disease of addiction. But his effort to "fix," to control things, only led to greater disaster for himself and his loved ones.

BEGINNINGS OF PROCRASTINATION

A third effect of the drug is to plant the seeds of procrastination and postponement that are a characteristic of all addicted people. If the future is now, all the addict has to do is get high and all plans—taking his children to the park, doing his laundry, bathing—are just as well as done merely by thinking about them. Remember, with the drug, nothing is impossible, nothing is difficult. It's only when the addict comes down from the high that he realizes that nothing is done and that the energy to do it now is progressively being eaten away. The tasks are postponed for a better time . . . a time that never comes.

Ellen, from the Midwest, was brought up to be ambitious, industrious, and serious about her goals. She wanted to be an architect, but life for Ellen wasn't all work and no play. During her college years, she learned how to smoke pot and drink margaritas as well if not better than the rest of them. A few mishaps occurred. She was involved in two minor car accidents, and had got herself in a situation that resulted in an abortion—all of this as a direct result of her excessive use and abuse of alcohol and drugs.

Fortunately, she finished her college course seemingly unscathed. Her parents were unaware of her questionable escapades, and the difficulties the drugs had put her in were all somehow ironed out with no embarrassing consequences. Most important, her future plans were clear. She would move to New York City, enroll at Pratt Institute, and land an entry-level job in her field. Naturally, she would share an apartment, since her funds would continue at the outset to be sparse.

Poor Ellen never got to the Registrar's Office, nor did she even search for an entry-level position. She did find an apartment. Unfortunately, it was a "share" with a girl whose boyfriend not only dealt drugs, but used the apartment to ply his trade.

During her very first week in the city, Ellen decided to postpone acting on her plans for one month. She would give herself one month to "adjust," as she put it, to her new environment.

At the end of that month, she was so well adjusted that not only was she progressing in her addiction, selling her body on orders of the boyfriend to the customers who passed through day and night, but considered her original plans to make no sense.

In Ellen's case, the first stages of physical addiction took hold of her life solidly and progressed rapidly. In one week's time, she decided to postpone her plan of action for one month. Within a short month, she had put it off for at least a year. It's been five years since that time. I am sad to report that Ellen is not yet better. She presently lives in a crack house. She appears gaunt and hopeless. She has aged beyond her years. When I would, on occasion, meet her on the street, she would tell me, "I'm rethinking my goals. I still want to go to Pratt. And I will, maybe next year. For now, though, there are many things that I need to do." The sad truth is that Ellen has nothing to do. She has lost her ability to choose. She has to continue to use.

LESSENING OF FEAR AND ANXIETY

The discovery of the drug lessens fear and anxiety. Above and beyond the small fears of living that plague all of us, the addict since childhood has lived with a fear of life that stems not from paranoia—a dysfunction of the emotions or of the brain—but a fear that has become part of his very being, of that part of him that is his identity. It is rightly called a spiritual fear.

What a freedom! It's like experiencing the loosening of the bonds that have strapped him for years. The drug destroys the paralysis of fear and worry and loosens the inhibitions, and finally our addict is able to leave his home, go out into the world, and be himself.

Alfred and I were college roommates. He came from a small Rhode Island town, and was extremely shy not only with strangers, but even with people he knew well. If he needed to ask me for something—like a pen or a piece of paper—he found it hard to ask for it. I, on the other hand, was more aggressive and forward. Even alone with me, Alfred was always content to let me make decisions and take initiatives. He was always very correct, and feared making a mistake, taking the wrong decision, or embarrassing himself.

As soon as he had a drink, Alfred loosened up and lost his inhibitions. One night both of us were visiting with a young married couple and decided to play cards. Drinks were served, and Alfred, in the course of the evening, had four scotches, while I opted for plain soda. His behavior instantly changed. He became talkative, hazarded a few awkward jokes that nonetheless made us laugh—I think less for their humor than from his unexpected aggressiveness and daring.

When it came time to leave, Alfred had to be coaxed to agree. I asked him for the keys to the car, saying that it would be dangerous for him to drive. To my surprise, he ridiculed my "unfounded fears." Very inappropriately, he began to attack me, telling me that "you are not as smart as you think you are," that "You always are so cocksure of yourself," that "I know better and I'm as able to drive as you are."

Later, Alfred went on to become a full-blown alcoholic, but is fortunately in recovery as I write this.

Another case in point was a neighbor of mine who was a still-functioning alcoholic and pill addict. She was a legal secretary and to all appearances a "together" person; she gave no indication of being in pain. As sometimes happens with addicted people, she developed an irrational fear of public transportation. Not wanting to drink alcohol before leaving the house in the morning for fear of being found out at the workplace, she would take two Valium pills. Instantly, her apprehension of the train ride vanished. It was just like magic.

There is also the classic story told by recovering people in the twelve-step programs about the little milquetoast addict in the bar who picks a fight with the biggest fellow in the house. The alcoholic and drug addict become liberated from fear. The drug gives them supercourage, and makes them behave in a way surprising to those who know them, including the addicts themselves. Their surprise ends in total confusion when later they can't understand why the big guy beat them up so badly.

FALSE HOPE

Finally, the discovery of the drug gives the addict hope. It is a hope that is basic and substantial. It is the hope that he, too, at last can maybe live like everybody else—carefree, creative, and even loving. For once, he can laugh . . . and cry. He feels more at one with the world than he ever did in his life. Little wonder that, upon being told that his problem is drugs, he denies it not only with a shake of the head but with a shake of his whole being—with his spirit. His denial is not only mental and emotional. It is a denial of his being that what you are telling him is unarguably wrong. And his experience proves him right. He feels lousy. Whammo! he takes a drug, and he feels good. Who can argue against that?

Unfortunately, this real hope experienced by the addict is false. How can it be otherwise? The hope is the product of an outside source of energy. It comes from something that has chemical reality but no human or spiritual reality. It is a setup for eventual despair.

At this point, the lie begins. The spirit is not properly identified. What the addict thinks is his human spirit, finally freed and able to breathe and function as he always wanted it to, is merely the effects (and short-lived at that) of the drug. The American Indians, upon discovering alcohol, deftly labeled it a "spirit." The pain prior to the drug is an unending sigh of the human spirit toward life and living, and the discovery of the drug is mistakenly identified as the realization of that goal.

At this point, the drug in reality doesn't work, because it makes the addict believe he is who he is not and believe he is not who he is. The addict genuinely thinks that his renewed zest for life is rooted in the real "him." This is the beginning of the lie, of the tragedy that spawns so much future pain for the drug addict.

This renewed hope in life is rooted *not* in the human spirit but in a chemical that has no spiritual or human reality. And the addict very quickly (almost immediately) recognizes this.

THE AWFUL REAL

For the alcoholic and for the drug addict, the next day—when he is in the throes of withdrawal, of a hangover, of a crash—it becomes cruelly obvious to him that he has been taken in . . . that he is a fool, that the seemingly authentic experience of the night before is not real, and he is crushed and confused.

Everything that took place during his revelry is not only a nightmare to him but absolutely and clearly something from which he wants to disassociate himself. The people he be- friended, he doesn't want to see. The money he squandered, which seemed so right to do at the time, now brings him shame. Even the remembrance of how good he felt makes him now squirm with a pain that only the experienced can fully comprehend.

The drug addict now feels, in a word, awful. So he does what seems to him to be the only possible thing for him to do. He has to continue to find a way out of his nonlife. He does so by dedicating himself in earnest to the drug of his choice. At the same time, he knows that something is wrong. He knows that the elixir is not the answer. He is therefore caught between the last possibility of hope that delivered for a time but sadly turned into pain and a still flickering love of life that now seems more and more impossible to attain.

The addict is demented. Confused emotionally and still rationalizing at full speed, he is demented in the pit of his being—his spirit. In the depths of him, he is becoming more and more convinced that there is something wrong with him—not on the surface, but in the depths of his being. His nature is wrong. Life has never played on his side of the court. He was always in battle against life . . . in order to survive and live himself. Always, life dealt him the bad blow. And even in the fleeting and apparently real experience of the drug, life once again slapped him in the face. What should work—and what is the only thing in the world that ever did work for him——isn't the perfect solution for him. Always an exception! Never for him! And now the addict is demented.

Unconsciously, he takes on the attitude of a warrior. And in effect, he declares war. Here, the insidiousness of this particular disease becomes apparent. He declares war against all and everything except the drug. If this disease were physical, our addict would be hostile to and blaming of the drug. If cranberries were the culprit, he would declare war against cranberries and swear off eating them for the rest of his life. But addiction is irrational. So, too, the addict. As a result, he aims his guns at all but the enemy.

He sets himself against people. Usually, he is most vituperative against the people closest to him and in time against all people. He sets himself against places. He hates his hometown, home state, his present place of residence, eventually the world at large. He sets himself against things. I remember my father, who had alcoholism. Once, as a youngster, I asked him why he had got drunk the night before. He replied, "It's because of that piano that your mother refuses to get rid of." My mother cherished her old upright, which her grandmother once owned and handed down to her. In my naïveté and my great desire to do anything in order to stop my father's drinking, I believed him and pleaded with my mother to get rid of the piano. She did. And guess what my father proceeded to do? You guessed it; he got drunk again.

Probably the last thing the addict turns against is the drug itself. While cursing the drug, the addict, in the same breath, ingests it. Consider the foul language and choice words the alcoholic uses to refer to his bottle and with which the drug addict refers to his drug. The latter calls it "dope" and "good s————." The former, "the f———— drink." At times, it is even possible to the experienced eye to observe the beginning of hate for the very drug that the addict now has less and less choice but to pursue. It is seen in his facial and body movements. Flashes of the yet-hidden truth of his soul are in his eyes, and deny what his hands are doing.

In declaring war, the addict arms himself with what I call "tools of defense." The tools that the addict takes on are the same as the tools used by the disease itself. They are lies, hate, concealment, denial, manipulation, violence, crime, and destruction of unlimited kind.

The spiritual deterioration that is described above is the focal point of the mental and the physical deterioration to come.

5

Spiritual Progression of the Disease

FROM THE SPIRITUAL point of view, the early stages of the disease are characterized by a hope that is false. As the disease intensifies and remains untreated, it enters the progressive stage. The results on the human spirit are twofold.

THE FULL FLOWERING OF FAITH

First, the addict, whether a believer or disbeliever, experiences a flowering of faith. Unfortunately, it, too, is false. Let me explain what I mean.

Suddenly, the addict becomes an expert philosopher. There is no more deep, hidden mystery or secrets to life. The addict has a theory for everything. Ask him anything on issues within and without the field of his expertise. Not only does he have the answer, but you damn well better agree with him. His is not only an opinion. It's the unarguable truth. I even suspect that a not-exceptional phenomenon takes place here. The disease robs him of his expertise, if ever he had one, and gives him the illusion of authority in all other matters. I further suspect that the disease itself leads the addict down the road of total error. It connects him with the lie of lies. It confirms his suspicion that a successful life requires one to know ... better still to know all things.

Unfortunately, this exhibition of superknowledge is accompanied by a growing alienation from and disdain for the power of the mind of the human being to know and probe beyond the sphere of acquired knowledge. More and more, the addict, parallel to his growing illusion of knowing all things, curses the human mind. He loses all respect for it, and considers it a burden more than a gift.

Norman, an acquaintance of mine, is a good example of this strange transformation. A brilliant man, he graduated from MIT as an aeronautical engineer. His professional career was equally brilliant, and he made a lot of money. Brought up a Roman Catholic, he eventually abandoned the faith of his childhood.

In the course of the years and on the occasion of my rare visits with him, we would discuss the religious question long into the night. Though not often able to agree with him, I couldn't help admiring the power and beauty of his scientific mind. He also, in the course of time, became an alcoholic.

Recently, I visited him in Arizona, where he presently lives. Now in his sixties, he is not the same person I once knew. His cynicism is universal, and he speaks of his well-honed intellectual formation as well as the power of the mind in derisive and downright pejorative terms. He remains antireligious, but now he is also anti-intellectual, and looks upon the powers of the human mind as another ploy of nature that played games with him only to make him the loser in the end.

Similarly, the addict becomes, if his temperament is so inclined, an expert politician. All of a sudden, he could do a better job than the mayor or the president. His union leader is inept, and the president of his tenants' association should be fed to the lions. At the same time, our politician curses the body politic and the very way of politics. While boasting of his command of politics, he proclaims the futility of embarking in that direction to better what is inevitably lost and not even worth saving.

In the area of religion or mere personal faith, our addict declares himself to be an atheist and curses life and nature. Or he declares himself a believer—the only sincere one—if only the world recognized it. At the same time, our friend curses God and all systems of belief.

This is the stage of the progression of the disease that brings the deep-seated failures of the addict to the surface. The virtues that they most lack are the ones they claim to be models of and boisterously boast about.

There is nothing so tragic as to witness a woman in a bar who in her addiction admits to being the vilest creature under the sun. But let no one question the quality of her motherhood! She will tell all present, in the midst of admitting the worst of mistakes and sins, that she is and always will be the best mother in the world . . . to the supportive applause of her fellow alcoholics. Meanwhile, her children are at home alone, unfed and neglected.

And the expert priest, minister, or rabbi who declares that he is the best clergyman in the world while failing to even show up on time for a scheduled religious service the following day. Or the expert locksmith who can't arrive on time for an appointed call, to the despair of the waiting customer.

In brief, the addict, at this point, is nothing unless he or she is an expert. But what is worse still is that the addict believes it. In fact, he believes everything at this point. Many a barroom brawl is caused by someone in the crowd who questions the sincerity and veracity of the drunk who extols his "beliefs." The liar becomes the victim of his own lie. He invents . . . and goes on to believe the invention.

To be mentally alert and still very feeling and to experience what I have just described is pure hell. The closest name, I imagine, that we have to express the pain of this disease is hell itself.

THE EXPERT LOVER

In the progression of this disease, we finally come to the ultimate level of development. If still unchecked, the addict experiences the biggest pain of all. He becomes the expert lover . . . but he, too, is false. The progression of the disease puts the addict in touch with the very reality that is slipping away from him. As he becomes incapable of loving or receiving love, he becomes acutely aware of its necessity, and at the same time of its absence in his life. To assuage the pain, he convinces himself that of all people he, alone, has the greatest ability to love and to receive love, if only there were someone capable of reciprocating.

We observe here *not* total lie and total hate. Rather, we observe the existence of a growing lie and of a growing hate that rests in a bed of genuine desire for truth and for authentic love. It is the paradox of this disease. More accurately, it is the contradiction inherent in this disease that the two realities exist side by side. Contrary to the nature of the paradox that brings together two things that apparently are dissimilar, the disease brings together in the addict two things that are in fact dissimilar and contradictory. As a result, the addict, though still real, is becoming more and more unreal. And, therefore, unspiritual.

If a believer, the addict here professes his knowledge and deep love of God. In the same breath, he literally hates God and expresses the depth of his defiance. He also professes his love of other people and things, and at the same time hates them so deeply that he physically wants to harm them and if possible destroy them. His respect for things has been lost. If he bumps into a piece of furniture, he damns it and wants to destroy it. At the height of his authentic claim of being an expert lover, his world is shrinking. He finds even less and less of himself. From the outset, the disease has eaten away at him from the inside. In his increasing isolation, he is angered that there, at the center of himself, he is no more. Born to be a creator of life, he has unwittingly become its determined destroyer.

HATE FOR THE DRUG AND FOR SELF

At the end of the evolution, the only thing left that doesn't walk away from him or that doesn't disintegrate at his touch is the drug of his choice. Yet, even though he doesn't abandon it but rather clutches it more jealously than before, he hates it more intensely than any nonaddicted person ever could. One has to be an addict to hate the drug to that degree.

Take, for example, the inveterate drug addict who is on his way to buy drugs. His face is hard and contorted. He is not in a mood for jokes. He can't laugh, because he is filled with hate for not only the drug that now is a need, but also for the seller to whom he will bow down and for whom he has the keenest of distrust. It is also the reason why the street alcoholic will clutch his now almost empty flask of wine, bring it to his lips, empty it, and, while giving it one more last look of despair, curse it before he hurls it through the air until it finally hits the concrete and breaks into a hundred pieces.

Now, the addict is in a corner. The disease has stripped him of everything. Even if people still stand by him, even if his job is intact, even if he has things, from the point of view of the diseased person, there is nothing left. Nothing, that is, except himself. When the addict looks there, he is repulsed by the sight. At this point, the mind is insane but still functioning, and the emotions are all distorted but also still functioning. As a result, when the addict looks inside himself, he does so with an ability to know and to feel, albeit with a sick mind and set of emotions. Fortunately, the spirit is still intact. Therefore, our sick addict lives on and can be helped. It is the unique wonder of addiction that recovery is always possible because nothing can touch the spirit, the very life of a human being—not illness, not death, not even addiction. As mentioned in the beginning of this book, addiction is a mysterious disconnection from life, but not an elimination of it. Once in recovery, the addict will find it there, unscarred, unhurt, and in as wonderful a condition as it was at birth. During the active stage of the disease, the addict is lost. He cannot find himself.

A woman drug addict revealed to me that one of the most painful experiences of her day was getting up in the morning and looking at herself in the mirror: "It was like I was looking at someone that I didn't know. Someone that I hated. Someone that I would rather die than have anything to do with!" She said this with an intense effort to find the exact words that weren't there to express her experience in accurate terms.

The only recourse, at this point, is *revenge*. From his point of view, the addict has lost the war on all fronts. So what does he do? He slips into despair and gives it to the world. If he can't have hope, then he will do all he can to see that nobody else has it. At this stage, he declares himself cursed, and so, too, curses the world and everybody in it. Better to not speak to the addict of optimism. He will hate you—if not punch you in the nose. Optimism causes him pain, and threatens his despair.

Another tool of revenge is *damnation*. Of course he knows that he is damned. By extension, he damns the world. Naturally, if he is damned, it follows that nothing and nobody is worth saving.

Finally, he wields his last tool of revenge—*death*. The addict wants to die. In fact, he is the "living dead." Contrary to statistics I have seen and opinions I have heard, it is not my experience that many addicts commit suicide. Other than the accidental overdose and the exceptional effective suicide attempt, all addicts only *desire* death. In most cases, it's the only desire they have left and that they can muster up. But few actually kill themselves.

Addicted people also wish death on everybody else for many reasons. "The person is no good; he is a born liar; never did a day's work in his life, etc. . . ." Ultimately, the addict wishes others dead because he is incapable of love—of saying yes to life, the gift of gifts.

I believe the human being is a spiritual being. As such, he survives in life by love. I firmly believe that if at any time the human being were to be without love, he would die. Love is the spiritual lungs of the human being, which I will discuss in the forthcoming chapters. At this time, I merely want to make clear that to be incapable of love and at the same time to be equipped with a life that is love—the very nature of which is to love—is to be in a tenuous position. In my opinion, it is to be in hell. That is why it is accurate to say that if someone wants to know what hell is like, all he has to do is to ask an addict in recovery. He's been there and back.

The spiritual effects of the disease of addiction as it progresses and reaches its inevitable bottom are grave. The initial, all-encompassing hope, the universal faith, and the unlimited love become at the end of the progression what they really were all the time—seeds of eventual despair, damnation, and death.

The addict is really not living. And to experience nonlife, with life still present, is the cruelest cut of all. It is a kind of pain that defies description. Only to have lived it is to really know it. Better to be dead than to be dead alive.

And the death of the spirit kindles the death of the mind, the feelings, and eventually the body. Addiction, in truth, is a killer. It is a fatal disease. Kill the spirit, and the body is sure to follow. We are, at this point, at the depths of the worst disease known to mankind—a disease worse than any other, because it attacks the outside from the inside. No area of life with which it comes in contact is safe from its destructive force. From the spirit of an individual, it penetrates every area of his being, his body, his mind, and emotive life.

And there is more. The disease contaminates whatever the sick person touches . . . not with his finger but with his love. That is why the family members and loved ones of every addict become sick with this disease. We call them codependents. There is no need for them to come in contact with the physical drug. These unfortunate victims need not be present when the addict plies his trade. Since the disease is spiritual, it is transmitted through a spiritual means—that is, a loving relationship with an active addict.

Bill, a childhood friend who grew up in an alcoholic home, told me that even when separated from his father physically, he could feel the pain while his father drank, just as if he were standing next to him: "One day I was ice-skating on a pond near my home with a group of boys. I was having a good time. All of a sudden, I left the ice and began taking off my skates. My friends wanted to know what was the matter and why was I leaving? I merely told them that I had to go home right away. Somewhere in my heart, I could sense that something at home was awry. Sure enough, I arrived home to find out that my father, after an argument with my mother, had gone out to get drunk. This premonition happened to me often."

As a result of this easy transmission, the codependent becomes sick spiritually. He, too, begins to disconnect from truth, from hope, and from the ability to live. As in the case of the active addict, he experiences a progression of the disease. Little by little, the spiritual dysfunction leads to mental, emotional, and physical breakdown.

The same Bill mentioned above confessed to me that by the age of five, he had already become an expert in fear and hate:

"I used to wait for the local bus with my mother. The bus stop was directly on the opposite side of the street of the local bar. Just seeing the bar, I wanted to throw a bomb at it. Also, the people that I saw going in and out of the bar, I wanted to kill. I hated them and judged them to be all bad people. Oh, yes! I could hate someone at five years of age without even knowing them or having met them.

"As for fear, I used to go to bed at my appointed time (I think it was seven-thirty P.M.) and curl up in fear while waiting for my father to come home. Even when he was home at bedtime, I still wouldn't let myself fall asleep for fear that a scene would develop and that he would again threaten my mother with getting drunk.

"This fear and negative state of being did a job on me. I was hypersensitive, easily hurt, and physically a nervous wreck!"

Rather than examining the significant problem of the codependent, I want to focus on the recovery from addiction. No doubt, addiction is incurable. It is tainted with social shame and condemnation. Worse yet, it attacks a person in his very spirit. But it is also the best of diseases. It carries with it the promise—no, the guarantee—of a recovery that lies beyond the limit of dreams.

It is to that hope of recovery that I wish to now turn.

6

Birth of Spiritual Sobriety— Life

LIFE OF THE BODY kindles life of the spirit. The self-help program of Alcoholics Anonymous likes to say, "Bring the body . . . the mind and the spirit will follow."

There is no question that the first effort to be made in the treatment of any disease called addiction is to treat the body. The physical aspect, although certainly not the heart of the matter, must be the first concern. When the baby is born, we first investigate its physical well-being. Then, and only long afterward, in fact, we probe its insides, its soul, its unique-ness—in a word, its spirit.

There is wisdom in Alcoholics Anonymous's answer to the newcomer's inevitable question: "What is the spiritual part of this program?" Alcoholics Anonymous replies, "Keep coming back. Just don't pick up, and the rest will follow."

Still it is my contention, based on observation of too many recovering addicts to count, that the invisible but real first experience in recovery is spiritual. Even before the addict is made aware of the wisdom of putting down the drug, he experiences what I call an "instinct of love." I believe that this initial and universal experience is God-oriented . . . or life-oriented, for people who do not adhere to any particular set of religious beliefs.

I have labeled this initial step to recovery an "instinct." This first experience of recovery is definitely not an act that is conscious and mentally controllable. Rather, I believe it is an impulse, a passionate movement of the soul toward life.

Fred, now a recovering alcoholic, told me the following tale:

"I woke up one morning in an awful state. I didn't want to live anymore. After dragging myself to the bathroom sink, I glanced up at myself in the mirror with total self-hate and disgust. Simultaneously, a deep feeling welled up in me, and I screamed at the mirror, 'God—if there is a God—help!' And then the tears came, and I couldn't stop crying.

"With hindsight, I look upon that moment with gratitude. It was the beginning of the thaw, the crack in the solid mass of pain that was to lead to my eventual delivery and recovery."

This instinct for life is from beginning to end a characteristic trait of the addict. Everyone knows that the addict parties well. Even in the course of an evening of fun, if he becomes ugly or depressed, it is easy for his fellow addicts to nudge him back into a partying mood. He is easily made buoyant again.

Another indication of the addict's love of life is found in his family. The family will tell you that, sober, he is the most lovable member of the family. They will say that he is a nice guy. "The nicest person you would want to meet," they will say. Or they will put it this way: "The most caring for us when the chips are down: I could always count on Johnny."

From my own personal experience, I can safely say that just knowing that he is an addict, I want to hug a person. I am sure that addicts are very loving people. In fact, I believe that is a requirement of addiction. I have yet to meet an addict who fails to meet this test. Addicts are good people, with a kinship for life and an instinct for love.

In one rehabilitation facility I worked in, a patient told me how pleasant and helpful all of his peers were. "Boy," he said, "I wish I had met up with these people when I was out there actively using!" He went on to say that his recovery thus far, without a doubt, more than any other therapeutic activity, was due to his interacting with the other addicts in the facility. They were getting each other better. The natural caring that characterizes all addicts was allowed to surface and was effectively doing its job of healing now that these addicts were drug-free and initiating their recoveries.

I did point out to the patient who brought this up to me that he need not regret not having met these same people while active. He certainly wouldn't have found them to be as "pleasant" as they were at the present time.

To sum up, a characteristic trait of the addict is an irrational love of life existing right alongside a growing despair of it.

Furthermore, love is the key to healing. When the cancer patient is told by his doctor that he has a limited time to live, the doctor is often heard to add, "It's all up to you now." What the doctor is saying is that if the sick person's desire to live is deep and live enough, he might be able to add some time to his life and even pull out of the danger zone that he is now in. In fact, we have seen time and time again that, even in matters of physical infirmities, the willingness to live, if strong enough in the sick person, can overcome all odds and lend the patient additional years of life. Cripples who are declared never able to walk again one day defy medical prophecy and begin to walk from the sheer spirit within them to heal and to live a healthy life. This last idea is best symbolized in the infant who, having barely scratched his finger, asks "Mommy" to kiss his "boo-boo" in order to make it all well. The mother kisses the hurt, and it goes away. Yes, love is life-giving, and it is healing.

And it is so even in its lesser forms. It is awesome to consider the power of love at work in human conception. Even when two people make love—that is, engage in physical love—a baby is born. This is true even in the case of two addicts who don't even know each other's names and are too "out of it" to connect with each other mentally and emotionally. The mere mutual physical acceptance or love of their bodies is powerful enough to produce a human being. The power of love, even in this lesser form, gives forth life.

I believe that it is this "instinct of love" that makes the addict cry out at one point in his addiction, "Help me! I want to live!" or more tellingly still, "Don't help me! I don't want to live!" This latter cry is more desperate. Although negative, it is more eloquent of a deep-down desire for help in order to live.

It is at the point of darkest despair, within the deepest confines of the being himself, that this primeval communion with anything healthy, positive, akin to life itself, takes place. Most of the time, the addict is not conscious of what is really going on. The cry mentioned above is sometimes screamed out to an empty room, a mute mirror. Other times it is just as loud but contained within. No matter, it is a first connection with truth.

I liken this experience to a kind of spiritual intercourse with whoever is there to hear. It is told to the world—to life itself—at the very moment when there is no one left to hear, there is no world, there is no more life for the addict. How can there exist for the addict anything on the outside, since he now is living the pain of nothingness on the inside? Even if there were something on the outside to hang on to, the addict has nothing within himself to connect with the outside.

I believe this experience is pure spiritual lust, comparable to physical lust, which operates by itself, above and beyond the will of the person engaged. This lust occurs despite the addict, very often unconsciously—certainly unwillingly.

I believe this impulsive cry that comes from the deepest part of the person is addressed to the inside God and, in the case of the atheist, to the life force itself. Furthermore, it happens in a moment of deep communion with oneself. It occurs at a moment when the addict is most connected, most in touch with his pain and with the part of the pain that hurts most deeply.

This feeble connection with a truth of the addict's life, albeit an ugly and a painful truth, is the humble beginning of love at work in the addict. Again, it is admittedly only a feeble connection with an ugly truth. Yet it is enough for the wheels of love to begin turning and to lead the addict to the next steps of recovery. It is the beginning and the harbinger of the healing to come. If nurtured properly, it will bring forth a beautiful baby full of promise and unlimited possibilities.

7

Instinct
of
Hope

LIFE IS MAINTAINED through uninterrupted connections. For example, once born, the baby needs to connect with living things. The baby is caressed in the warm arms of hospital personnel. He is held lovingly by his mother and father. In the arms of the living, the baby's own life is maintained and nurtured. In the same way, throughout the process of recovery, beginning with its initial step, the first connection of love maintains itself and increases as more connections are made.

The second step in the process of recovery is other-oriented. The spiritual connection described in the last chapter takes place within the person with life itself. To survive, the inner life needs to be connected with life from without. This second step in the process is a manifestation in the visible world of what transpired and took place in the very real but uncontrollable and invisible world—in that place where dwells the very mystery of the individual human being.

In other words, the cry "Help me!," if effective, must be connected to life closest to the addict outside of him. And where on the outside of the addict is the reality endowed with most life to be found? The answer, of course, as with the newborn, is in another human being.

Who might this other person be? It could be anybody, depending on the circumstances of one's life. It could be a friend, a family member (rare), a co-worker, a bartender, a counselor, a psychiatrist, maybe even a pure stranger. The circumstances of the connection are as varied as there are addicts. Sometimes the communication is made through a telephone call, a simple admission on the part of the addict that he hasn't yet surrendered, speaking out in an outburst of anger for the first time, a moment of crying, a moment of truth in treatment.

Sometimes the logistics of this second connection are long and circuitous. It sometimes takes a month, a year, or several years for the connection to come full circle and produce its fruit. If the addict doesn't lose heart, if he continues to share his own truth—namely, his need and desire for help—his cry will eventually fall on ears that will give him the life-giving response.

A recovering alcoholic tells the following story:

"Around ten o'clock one morning, at a time when I was in total despair, I picked up the phone and called two longtime friends. One lived in Canada, and the other in a neighboring state. In both phone calls, the conversation was very brief because I could hardly speak. I was in such a state that had I wanted to speak at length, I wouldn't have been able to. I told both friends that something was wrong and that I needed help.

"Within the hour, I received a call from one of them, who informed me that they both would come and spend a week with me in the city where I then lived. They came, and I was as honest as I could be with them, because my desire to feel better was so great. Of course, I made no mention of alcohol or drugs to them, simply because I was certain that those things had nothing to do with my problems. For godsake! At that point in my life, alcohol was the only thing that made me feel better. How could *it* be *the* problem?

"At the end of the week, and because neither of my friends was able to find a solution, they suggested that I consult a psychiatrist. Although reluctant at first, I finally agreed, and pulled out the name of a doctor from the Yellow Pages of the local telephone directory.

"After I'd been seeing this psychiatrist for about seven months, he suggested that I attend meetings of Alcoholics Anonymous. This suggestion was the result of my attending a session with him completely intoxicated. I objected by arguing that, although I probably had a problem with alcohol, I wasn't surely an alcoholic. He responded by telling me to go to these meetings in order to find out and make sure. Finding no objection with which to counter his argument, I agreed and attended my first meeting.

"Of course, I didn't speak with anyone at the meetings, and didn't encourage anyone to speak to me. After about six months of this, I began to feel very isolated, and a failure in Alcoholics Anonymous. I finally concluded that this program wouldn't work for me. I also felt that the members there spoke a lot about extending their hand to newcomers and of brotherly love. However, I failed to see any practice of those lofty ideals where I was concerned. And I became very angry.

"While in a meeting one night, I decided that I wouldn't

return to Alcoholics Anonymous. As I was lost in my own thoughts, a man sitting next to me nudged me in the ribs. I looked up and saw everybody turned around and looking at me. The girl leading the meeting simply told me that it was my turn to speak if I wished to.

"Taken by surprise, I did the very thing that, if time to think had been given, I would never had done. I opened my mouth and spoke. I expressed my anger and disappointment with them, and added that I would not be returning to meetings anymore.

"At the end of this little harangue, the girl in charge simply said to me, 'Jeff, because you spoke tonight, your life will change.' And, boy, did it change! After the meeting, many members came to greet me and gave me their phone numbers. They even took me to a coffee shop, where I stayed till two in the morning, telling them what I hadn't been able to share with another human being for nearly forty-two years.

"Already, my life was changing!"

The above story demonstrates the long and sometimes twisted path that the connections involved in the process take. Taken out of context and isolated, most of the connections that Jeff had to experience would be misleading and not clearly related to solving his problem and thereby opening him up to life.

If any addict walks this road, it seems to me that he will experience the guarantee of recovery that is his right. His spiritual cry for help necessarily will result in life at a time no one can predict but perfect for every addict.

More specifically and immediately, it will lead to a surrender *of* the old and a surrender *to* the new.

The surrender of the old means, first and foremost, the drug. Second, it means all the "buts." When the addict says,

"I would stop using drugs but . . . ," one must beware. At this juncture, the addict himself is forewarned and is called to surrender whatever follows that word "but."

It could mean a surrender of God if for one particular addict he would surrender the drug but for the fear and guilt he has of God who is waiting to exact just retribution for his sinful life. It could mean that the addict's particular code of morality, as he has tried to live it, is an obstacle to being able to put down the drug and to surrendering it unconditionally. Some of you will say, "How can God and morality—such seemingly rightful things—be obstacles to a man's sobriety?" We must not forget that this disease is so insidious that, without warning, it uses the best of things to keep the addict entrenched in his addiction. It can use mother, child, money, God, and the moral code to drive the addict right back to his drug of choice. Mere discomfort concerning all these good things of life are signals to the recovering addict that, however desirable they are in themselves, he must reluctantly surrender them for a greater good—the salvation of his own life. First to live, then to believe in God, then to serve Him, and then to be moral. But first to live.

A friend of mine, addicted to both alcohol and drugs, shared the following experience of his life in recovery with me:

"I was about one month sober and clean. I was not yet able to work. However, my recovery friends had seen to it that I was kept busy. If not attending meetings, I was at one or the other's house having coffee and speaking at length about recovery. But, one day, I finally found myself with nothing to do. I decided to go to a rather sleazy part of town, and slipped into an X-rated movie.

"Upon returning home, an anxiety and sense of failure gripped me. Up to then, I had really been a very moral person in my recovery time. What else! I had been kept too busy to give myself to anything that I considered morally wrong. As a result, I was disappointed with myself, and I felt like a failure. Thank God, I had the brains to call a recovering friend, and shared my escapade with him.

"After hearing the details of what had occurred, he interrupted and asked me if I had picked up a drink or a drug. I replied that I hadn't. He immediately told me that because I hadn't picked up any form of drug, all was okay.

"I couldn't believe him, but somehow took his word and acted on it. If I hadn't done so, I see today with hindsight that the moral preoccupation that I had could have become so worrisome and painful that I could have resorted once again to my drug of choice for relief. And I would have been off to the races again!"

Other "buts" that the addict can be called to surrender are his family, his relationship, his job, his career, himself, his vacation plans, his friends—all and whatever weakens his resolve to surrender the old way—the way of drugging instead of the way of living in truth and in the real.

Not only does this second step in recovery require the addict to surrender the old, it also requires him to surrender *to* the new. This surrender to the new is a surrender to another human being. For once in the addict's life, he is going to share himself not with a drug but with another human being—with someone alive and for whom he has longed all his life. He is going to choose a person who is sympathetic to his disease and to the steps of recovery. To this person, the addict will eventually reveal all of his secrets. This process is beneficial to his healing because it is another form of connection. Little does the enormity of what he shares and reveals matter. What is healing is that he shares it. The miracle of healing comes in the connection that is made. Even if the feedback given is irrelevant or vacuous, it matters little. Life is restored through the connection.

Barbara, a middle-aged woman who is recovering from alcoholism, told me how she first got started in Alcoholics Anonymous:

"For six months, I attended meetings. I was still unable to identify with the people as an alcoholic. I hadn't gotten a breakthrough yet. And I kept drinking. Yet every time I returned home from a meeting, I did so with a light heart. I was astonished at how the people there would share how they were feeling with one another—with strangers, really. All my life I had searched for a place in the world where I could speak of myself in all honesty, without fear of reprisal and of being judged. I had even joined a church-sponsored organization in the hope of finding just that. But even within that group, I shortly found out that it was not possible without negative results.

"Still, how I yearned to have what those people seemed to have! You know, that yearning kept me going back to the meetings. Thank God! By returning to the meetings, I finally became able to approach someone and haltingly speak to her. She eventually became my sponsor (a guiding friend in the twelve-step programs) and I began to share and to heal. I stopped drinking that very day."

Second, the addict surrenders to a group of people. It isn't that he is going to connect his innermost thoughts to this group. That, he does with another human being. But the addict is a social animal. He also needs to rub elbows, albeit on a social level, with a host of different people. In this way, he becomes more polished and finds the real sparkle that is his own. Here, the social interaction made possible by meetings and gatherings of self-help programs such as Alcoholics and Narcotics Anonymous is of inestimable value.

Finally, he surrenders to another new reality. He surrenders to a caring God. This is not the old God who was after him, who gave him shame, who consistently built obstacle after obstacle in his life. This God is on his side. He is the one who loves him just as he is: in his sin as well as in his addiction. He is the God who patiently waited for him to open his arms, to say yes, to stop trying to find him. It is a God, finally, whom the addict happily admits he does not know, but with whom he connects. Even the atheist, with time, can come to welcome such a God, if and when He should ever make himself known. Finally, it is a God who in the worst of circumstances loves the addict before the addict asks him to, before the addict even begins to wonder if He does.

This second connection in the process of recovery is one of trust. The addict, in blindly establishing it, is already rewarded with a fuller life: another human being, a group of people, and a caring God. His world is being populated not with illusions, false people, and hallucinations, but with truth, reality, and loving people.

How easy it is then, thinks the addict to himself. His pain begins to dissolve. He could hardly believe it himself if he were not experiencing what at first he couldn't understand or believe. The taking of this second step in the process of recovery is for the recovering addict a spiritual experience. It lies not in the mind, in the belief, in the feelings, but in the doing.

8

*Instinct
of
Faith*

IT IS A FACT as old as life itself that we first become aware of the outside of things before the inside. The baby once again is a good example of this phenomenon. As the process of growth takes place, the baby little by little turns inward to contemplate himself. He first discovers his body—his outside self. He then connects with his feelings, his imaginings, and his thoughts. In last place, and only if fortunate enough to reach a desirable maturity, he discovers his soul—the part of him that is spirit.

Again, the disease of addiction is very much a spiritual disease. It is a disease of life. Consequently, its devastation is centrally located in that place where life is found in us. To reverse its direction—that is, to recover—one must replay the experience that took place from birth on. At the beginning, the process was unconscious. With time, it surfaced into consciousness. In the recovery of addiction, the same process takes place. The instinct of love is an unconscious experience—not conjured up by the individual. It occurs spontaneously, independent of the addict's will and intention. The consciousness awakens, and the hopeless addict asks for help. The response, indirect as it sometimes may be, is inevitably loud and clear. It is a promise of help and a guarantee of hope even for him—the addict—who considered himself hopeless.

With that, we embark on the third stage of recovery. This is where the addicted person is told the truth about himself. For the first time in his life, he is told that he is powerless over alcohol and drugs.

In the beginning of the recovery process, the addict established first a communication, a connection with God (life inside of himself, for those who don't believe in a God). Second, he connected with the world around him, with life outside of himself—another human being. Now, he is ready to establish a deep, spiritual connection with himself.

This connection is beyond any other the addict has ever known. It is a knowledge that surpasses all previous knowledge that he has had about himself. It goes beyond the knowledge of his name, his way of being, his tastes, his dislikes, his way of feeling, or his way of thinking. The addict now receives, as a gift for the connections he made with life and with his peers, the knowledge that he is powerless. It is a truth that penetrates beyond anything that the human being could ever know about himself.

He receives the communication and the impetus to admit, to accept, that he is powerless over drugs physically, mentally, and spiritually. Physically, because his body can't take drugs; they have become a poison to his system as it is constituted.

Mentally, because his mind and his feelings cannot handle drugs; the addict becomes nonfunctional, or rather falsely functional, not only when the drug is ingested, but even when the drug is merely contemplated prior to ingestion. And finally, spiritually, because the drug once in the body disconnects the person from his very spirit—from the thing in him that makes him alive and that gives him life . . . his very self.

But there is more. As a direct consequence of his making the two first connections—with life and then with a human being—the recovering addict is told a still deeper truth about his nature. The addict is told that not only is he powerless over the drug, but that he is powerless over God and life, over others, and over other things. Finally, he is told that he is powerless over even himself. In learning this liberating truth, he is urged with love and caring to admit it and make it his own—to connect with it as he connected with his pain.

Why is the concept of powerlessness so essential to the question of spiritual recovery from addiction? Very simply put: because powerlessness is so essential to physical recovery. We can't *know* spiritual realities. They are beyond our grasp. Our only access to the spiritual is through the physical—the only level of reality that we can know by seeing and touching. Remember, the disease is not in the drug. Rather, the drug is the symptom, the outward and visible sign of the real problem, which is found within the individual. Since the addict becomes physically sick from use of the drug, he gets to find out that he is sick inside from something else. In the case of the drug, the addict begins to recognize that it is a tool that allows him to exercise power and control. If the addict gets up in the morning and fears the day, all he has to do is pop a pill or down a drink, and the problem is *fixed* for the moment.

Eventually, the addict begins to recognize that as long as he attempts to *fix* his life—that is, to exercise control over it—he rapidly begins to lose it.

This experience with the physical drug mirrors what is going on spiritually—in the depths of his soul. As long as the addict tries to better his life with his own power—to control events and people, including his very self, how he feels, etc., he will find himself slipping away from life and away from the comfort and happiness that he craves.

On the other hand, once he allows himself to experience powerlessness over the drug, he experiences a new freedom— an ability to go through a day without it—something that he never dreamed possible. Again, that physical ability to be without the drug and still feel better mirrors what will happen to his life if only he applies the same powerlessness to all things—events, people, and himself. He will become spiritually free on the inside, and life will once again—as when he was a baby—begin to work by itself as it is made to do. But he has to get out of his own way and leave it alone. In this respect, I heard a member of Alcoholics Anonymous exclaim, "Life is now none of my business. All I have to do is show up for it!"

Yes, powerlessness is not helplessness. I must "show up for it." That means I must make myself present to it. It means living to the fullest, using all of my faculties and talents to let life then determine the result. The baby is totally powerless. Yet how it grows! And it grows precisely because it doesn't try to substitute itself for life. Rather, it removes itself and allows life, however it presents itself, to take charge.

Power, only because it is suspicious of life—the source of power—leads to less life and ultimately to death. Addiction is an excellent case in point.

At this juncture in the recovery experience, we have gone full circle. We have gone from addiction to recovery—from death to life.

This third phase of recovery is by all means meaningful. It is the door that opens up the addict to all of the recovery experience as it enfolds in time. For it is only when the individual takes consciousness of utter powerlessness in the midst of all creation that he is able to be aware of his real destiny—to be the king of creation.

Allow me to explain what I mean. Have you ever wondered about the status of man and woman in a world so frightening and so fraught with constant danger to body and soul? The human species is by far the most vulnerable of all created reality. Humans are more vulnerable than the insignificant ant that can hide in his well-made canals far under the earth's surface—more vulnerable than any other creature endowed with life. The lion is stronger, the lynx sees in the dark, and the rabbit runs faster.

Not only are all the species of the animal kingdom superior to man in one area or the other, but the natural forces, usually so benign and friendly, can without prior warning become killers and remain beyond the vain attempts of man to harness and to control.

Yet it is not the wind, the fire, or the earth itself—it is not the lion, the lynx, or the pink-eyed rabbit—that were made the stewards of creation. It was man—the most fragile of all created things.

There is a lesson in that. It is a lesson that our beloved addicts in this world have a golden chance to learn if ever they embark on the road to recovery from their deadly disease. The lesson is that all people who qualify as human are by nature, by will of the Creator, made powerless. It is the very specificity of the human species to be powerless. The intention here is not to make humans helpless—to keep them underfoot, as it were. Rather, powerlessness is a necessary requirement to enjoy the destiny reserved to mankind.

The human being is in a very pointed and exclusive way destined to love. In order to carry out that function and that mission, the human being must be equipped with the necessary tools. The ultimate tool of love is found in the rare art of being powerless—of not exercising control.

Life is that way. It plays without power. That is why it is never bothersome. Everything else in life can bother us, and at various times attempts to have power over us—people, events, the weather, even the typewriter that I am writing on or the very expensive automobile that I am driving can determine the events of my day, depending on whether they function properly or not.

As a result, it can be said that the real power is this world is powerlessness—freedom to love, freedom to be "me" with no one and nothing getting in the way. And everything gets in the way, doesn't it? Money, relationships, sex, and at times even religion can at a surprising moment in life stop me in my tracks from being fearless and fully alive.

Incidentally, that is also why our prayers that petition God to exercise power and to fix our lives seemingly are never answered. Every alcoholic and addict that I know eventually gives up on prayer for that very reason. His life never gets fixed. Rather, it gets worse. And so the addict feels that God has given up on him.

Yet all the great religions say that mankind's prayers, in fact, are always answered. "Ask, and it will be given to you; search, and you will find; knock, and the door will be opened to you. For the one who asks always receives; the one who searches always finds; the one who knocks will always have the door opened to him. Is there a man among you who would hand his son a stone when he asked for bread? Or would hand him a snake when he asked for a fish? If you, then, who are evil, know how to give your children what is good, how much more will your Father in heaven give good things to those who ask him!" (Matthew 7:7–11). The holy Koran says, "And be steadfast in prayer and regular in charity; and whatever good ye send forth for your souls before you, ye shall find it with Allah; for Allah sees well what ye do." (Sura II:110). The same idea is expressed throughout the Jewish tradition. "Study the generations long past and understand; has anyone hoped in the Lord and been disappointed? Has anyone persevered in his fear and been forsaken? Has anyone called him and been rebuffed? (Sirach: 2:10). And I, too, believe that our prayers are always answered. The only prayer that cannot be answered is the one that seeks to unleash and to exercise power. That prayer, if answered, would alter or destroy the very essence of the human being, which is all powerlessness and love.

In brief, the relationship that life and God have with us is one of love and caring. It is a gift that makes us precious and, as a result, all the more fragile and powerless.

One of addiction's many lies and tools of destruction is to rob us of our ability to connect with the very essence of our natures, of who we are. That is why, when the disease finally becomes physical and visible, we witness the transformation of the person whom we thought we knew. The physical connection with the drug changes the person. The change is, in its progression, almost complete. Of course, the personality changes ... but down the road even the face, the features of the body, undergo a gradual transformation such that, even in their bodies, addicts become at first sight unrecognizable by the very people who know them well.

The function, the reason why the human being was made, is to love. It certainly isn't to brush teeth, to work, to raise children, wash clothes, or go to the movies. Surely, we do all of these things, but they are not the final end of why we were put here on earth. In themselves and in the long run, they could hardly make and keep us happy. Instead, the only justification for all other realities and activities is love. Love makes it all worthwhile and gives meaning to our otherwise drab and in themselves meaningless activities and existence.

Upon hearing this revelation for the first time, the addict, in the early stages of recovery, doesn't comprehend. He remembers that he always did feel powerless. In fact, powerlessness was one of the problems of his life. Remember, the experience of addiction is the fear and the slow actualization of the fear that one won't make it, that one will fail.

And now, the addict hears himself being told that he is in fact powerless—that he has failed. He is told to face the failure, the defeat, and to surrender to it. He is even urged to state it, to declare it, to make it the very slogan and foundation of his recovery—the bedrock upon which a recovered life will blossom and bring forth life eternal. The addict is asked to admit that he is powerless over the drug and powerless over life. What a grace! . . . he is told.

And it *is* a grace. The connection with his truth is the key—the one the addict looked for since consciousness. It is the key that will open the door to a life that always works, that even works by itself . . . only because the person doesn't get in the way, doesn't try to make it work, doesn't try to exercise power and control over it. Life becomes recalcitrant and ceases to operate as soon as it is not left free to work according to its own law.

Mankind, which is sent out to dominate the world, is surely well equipped to do it. We are given the gift of gifts. We are given life—a life that never fails, a life that always gives results and becomes more and more abundant. Alongside and part of that gift, mankind is given a vulnerability—we can now call it a powerlessness—that is the assurance and the guarantee that we will not interfere with the process of our gift and that our gift will be effective.

And to be grateful to have the addiction, this frightful disease, is to make the following statement: "I am a grateful recovering addict because at the very moment that I erred, that I tried to make the gift work, the gift itself bucked and floored me, until I became convinced that surely there had to be another way."

The path of recovery is the "other" way. To recognize through a pain so deep and so substantial that one is powerless, then to admit defeat and be open to suggestion, and finally to declare one's powerlessness, at first on the word of one better versed and experienced but then on the basis of one's own experience, is a grace indeed. It is a grace that the recovering addict explores for the rest of his life.

If that power that explains the infallibility of life itself is not mine to wield or my responsibility to answer to, that power must exist elsewhere. At this point, the newly recovering addict is told to submit—to allow a power outside himself to restore him to reality (the seat of sanity). He finally is directed to let that power, whatever it might be, take over and manage his life.

In fact, this is a relief—or should be—to the recovering addict. Most of the time, the prospect of putting his life in the hand of an unknown power is frightening. When one looks closely at the burden and pain that the addict endured all of his life to make life work, it follows that a sense of relief should accompany such a suggestion. It doesn't immediately unburden the addict only because he has shouldered that responsibility for so long that he is no longer aware of the heaviness and the destructiveness it has continued to cause him along the way.

In time, provided the recovering addict is willing, the wisdom of such a decision will be revealed to him. Not only will he know a relief, but he will be healed and at last be made able to live.

9
Spiritual Progression of Recovery

NOW THAT the recovering addict is a functioning human being again, now that he has connected with life within himself and with life around him (his proper nature and destiny), the road to growth in recovery is wide open and without limit.

This unlimited characteristic of recovery should come as no surprise when one reflects on the experience of the disease itself. One hears with frequency recovering alcoholics and addicts speak of "having hit my bottom." In general, this "bottom" refers to the moment in their addiction that was the most painful . . . in fact, so painful that it motivated them to seek help.

Perhaps the story of Susan, whom I first met in a treatment

center and more recently ran across, best illustrates this wretched experience.

"Things began," she admitted, "at my bottom, to lose their worth, their consistency. Even the drug wasn't working anymore. It just seemed to give me more pain. If only I could have been certain that life and living wouldn't get any worse. But the fear and the experience was that it was always getting worse. There didn't seem to be any end to it. That's why I wanted to die and would just as soon have been dead. But even the thought of death was less and less consoling. It just added to the despair."

For certain, the pain experienced in addiction is such that one reaches "bottom" only to find that there is no "bottom." Rather, the disease leads to a bottomless pit. Hence, the indescribable despair.

Similarly, the experience of reclaiming one's life is without ceiling. It is without end. Recovery from this disease is not a recovery from some physical ailment like smallpox wherein one recovers a smoothness of skin. Nor is it a recovery from a mental incapacity in which one becomes able to distinguish sanity from insanity. Rather, it is a recovery from a spiritual disease in which one is in the process of reclaiming one's very life. Like life, this recovery defies constriction, limitation, and a priori dimensions of any kind. Like life, it is eternal and infinite. It is the real hope, finally, of an echo that the addict has heard in the bowels of his soul, however faintly, since birth—an echo that made him know beyond knowledge that his gift was without limit and that he was made to have it all. In a very real sense, the real hope of recovery is found in the real possibility of finally becoming the god that his nature calls him to be. "Called to be the sons of God . . . and true heirs of the Kingdom . . ." (Romans 8:14–17). At last the recovering person sees the reality of his calling. It is a call to be the recipient of life, first; and then to be the giver of life. The human being, through the experience of living out his humanity—which includes life at its worst—becomes, in a word, divine. He becomes the god of his world!

To speak of the progression of what I call spiritual sobriety is not easy. As for all things spiritual, there exist no accurate words. Allow me to speak around the concept with the only words that I have.

When considering spiritual sobriety, I reflect on those things that make for the most perfect happiness that man can imagine. They consist of those realities that answer to the secret yearnings of the human heart—those yearnings that never leave us, that are always present, however much they seem out of reach most of the time.

From personal experience, I believe that life, to be whole and fully nurturing, must be creative, exciting, loving, and humble. Not surprisingly, these four ingredients are observed to be the main arteries around which growth in recovery takes place and thrives. This growth does not occur instantaneously. It is gradual and progressive—like a journey in which one advances mile after mile toward the desired destination.

A CREATIVE
JOURNEY

The addict on his way to growth in recovery gradually but surely is opened up to the possibility and the desire to be creative. Creativity is without a doubt something that stems from life. Biologically, it is demonstrated in the ability to give birth, to form and to mold. It is also demonstrated in the natural growth of the body itself.

This biological fact is a physical symbol of the more real ability and nature of the human spirit. To want to extend itself in the form of another being, another life—in the form of more life—is proper to human nature.

As a result, the recovering addict finds his life becoming more creative in various ways. First, his life becomes more personal. Contrary to the past, his actions, thoughts, and decisions are less based on outside influences and more on the inner truth that makes up the unique person that the addict is. His behavior becomes more and more an expression of the reality of his being—of his mystery. Actions are based on who *I* am, and not on what others or society or family or even God expect me to be.

Ruth, after one year in recovery, became aware that she was an inveterate people-pleaser. She couldn't say no! One day, at work, her boss told her to check the photocopier. It wasn't working properly. Ruth, who in the past would have spent close to a fretful hour trying to fix the machine, simply told her boss, "I'd love to accommodate you. However, I have a fear of machines and would much prefer if you gave someone else the assignment." The boss beamed back with a smile on his face: "Oh! You're like me! Not handy with machines! I can sympathize. Never mind, I'll get Andy to take a look at it." Ruth was stunned, and as a result of her self-assertion and honesty, felt more pleased with herself than she had for years. Since then, Ruth has become more enthusiastic in seeking to be who she is.

Another aspect of the personal characteristic of the recovering life is that, in the disease, the spiritual, mental, and even the physical get to be the same. Addicts all talk about the same things in the same way; they react the same way to human situations; their life patterns come to be the same; after a while, they even look the same physically. They all have the addict look, giving validity to the often-heard statement. "He looks like an alcoholic . . . a drug addict." Mentally, the same phenomenon takes place. Active addicts talk the same "rap." They try to manipulate others with the same stories of their "varied problems" with job, school, relationships, and, especially, money. Their conception of life, of the world, and of other people—including their families—is usually negative and pejorative. They seek each other out to share the same way of thinking, often in a vocabulary that is unique to them. Finally, and from the spiritual point of view, they are all unsure, afraid, totally in the lie and unable to love.

That is why in the twelve-step recovery programs all of the personal stories, as varied as they seem to be, basically say the same thing. At meetings of Alcoholics Anonymous, for example, it is only those in attendance who are still close to the disease who find an element of difference in the stories they hear. For the seasoned member, nothing in the stories surprises him. In truth, the stories at times can get boring. That the newcomer finds them enjoyable is in part due to the insidiousness of the disease. In fact, this insidiousness made the addict throughout his illness feel that his situation was unique. Part of recovery helps the addict to recognize that the time he found himself to be most different was when he was most like all of the other addicts around him.

In recovery, this sameness little by little gives way to a growing difference in the physical, mental, and spiritual makeup of the individual life. What is happening is that the addict in recovery is connecting more and more with the reality of his being and discovering its uniqueness and individual richness.

Death is sameness, and life is difference. As the disease becomes more pronounced, the sameness surfaces and takes hold. As the recovery progresses, the differences emerge. We see how inevitably as the addict recovers, he becomes a more sought-after person simply because he is allowing his true self to express itself. Consequently, he becomes more original and interesting to other people. This phenomenon is a complete reversal of attitude. In the past, the addict tried to hide his real self for fear of being found dull and uninteresting to his peers.

The creative experience in recovery is therefore personal. It is also free. At last, the spirit of the person is in charge. And the human spirit can exist and function only in a free atmosphere. No more does the addict do things or say things because he "must." The addict's behavior is always predicated on choice. "I choose to do this or that." As a result, the addict is now open to risks. The addict can "try" things to see if they fit the kind of person he really is. And what if it should prove to be a mistake? No fear. In recovery, the addict is now free to make mistakes, knowing that he is never stuck. In the disease, a mistake was fatal—or near-fatal— every time. In recovery, a mistake is merely a learning experience that serves to advance the addict on his proper road.

In this regard, Joe, a friend of mine who has a few years of recovery under his belt, had entertained the idea of beginning a spirituality center for recovering people. In his personal encounters as well as his observation in the meeting rooms of recovering people, he noticed a need and a desire that they had for spiritual growth. He felt that a center where people could go at will and at their leisure would answer that need.

Finally, one day, he approached his sponsor and shared his idea with him. In doing so, he expressed his fear that maybe he was being grandiose and that the idea was really beyond his ability to pursue. He therefore forthrightly asked his sponsor if he thought that his idea smacked of grandiosity. The sponsor's simple but telling reply was, "Try it and find out." The implication of the comment made by this sponsor was that if the idea should turn out to be unrealistic, a mistake, Joe would first get the experience of it and then find out. Meanwhile, nothing would be lost and a lot gained. In this context, even mistakes made in recovery serve the addict well.

Finally, the experience of recovery in progression is creative because it is artistic. To be a human is to be an artist. To have life is to give life. To be alive is to be creative.

The role of the active disease (which is why addiction is so destructive and fatal) is to attempt not to lose life by keeping it, by seeking to hoard it, by taking chemical substances that will ward off all loss. As a result, the life lessens, weakens, and dies. In recovery, the trick is to discover that life survives on the gift of self. Life gives life, and in that way maintains itself and grows.

In this creative experience of recovery, the addict finds himself and his own path. He creates his own life. What nature did for him as a child, he now does for himself in a conscious way. The greatest work of art, even for the recognized artist, is to find the pieces of his own life and create the unique pattern that he is. This is the experience of the recovering addict.

There is more to me than what you see. I will show you. It will take me a lifetime. It's the old story of "Little Red Riding Hood." The author of this piece of children's art was a genius.

And he was an artist. He took less to make more. He took what he had in hand, and with it made something that wasn't there before.

What is the process inherent in the birth of this nursery tale? What, for that matter, is the process found at the bottom of every great work of art? The artist, in every case, takes something real that is at hand, and by putting it together in a way that is unique and original produces something that didn't exist before.

The tale of "Little Red Riding Hood" demonstrates this very well. The author took known and controllable bits of reality, such as a little girl with a red cape, a basket of lunch, a house, a wooded area, a wolf, and a grandmother. Through his artistry, he has created ways that make these mute items express a truth that otherwise we could never communicate to the child. These items combined in a certain way reveal to the child that there is evil in the world.

In the Judeo-Christian view of the world, this kind of artistry is at the basis of creation. God took what He had (He had nothing, says the Bible), and with it He made the world.

It is also the experience of the addict in recovery. The addict slowly learns to trust enough in life so that he begins to take the imperfect and seemingly defective elements that he has and, with them, begins to build a life. And what a product it turns out to be! There is no limit to what can result. It opens him to unlimited possibilities. He no longer feels incapable of making something out of his life. His problem now is to choose a path. So many possibilities are open to him that he is faced with the dilemma of choice . . . of varied possibilities. Whatever his decision, he can be certain in recovery that the mansion the artist chooses to build will be beautiful and one-of-a-kind.

AN EXCITING JOURNEY

The life of the recovering addict is certainly creative. And because it is creative, it is necessarily exciting—the second ingredient or characteristic of someone who is progressing in the recovery from addiction.

How else could life be but exciting when one comes in contact with one's nature and in so doing with nature itself? What an ecstasy to discover that one is called to be a creator of self in order to become a creator of others.

For certain, as much as life for the active addict is one big blob of boredom, life in recovery is anything but that. In fact, one of the enemies of recovery is boredom. A boredom that maintains itself over a period of weeks cannot be ignored by the recovering addict if he wishes to maintain his recovery. Boredom that takes root in the very fabric of life itself is a danger sign, and must be investigated and ultimately resolved.

I say the above not to be overly aware of danger but only because life itself *is* exciting and, as such, is incompatible with boredom. If it's boring, it's not life—or I am not living when faced with something that I experience as boring. Boredom cannot coexist with life.

On the contrary, life is exciting. It is constant change and variety. That is why life never duplicates itself. In fact, it abhors duplication. To date, Nature has never produced two identical leaves. In human reproduction, it can be said that identical twins are a misnomer. The mother knows the difference. The twins themselves are extremely conscious of it also.

Life is open to everything. Experiences that the addict couldn't warm up to or develop an interest in all his life can become appealing. From hating music, he begins to take guitar lessons; from never going to a movie, he begins to become a movie buff; never an outdoorsman, he finds he loves weekends camping in the mountains; the variety of activities that the addict discovers in recovery are endless. He was unaware of these newfound pleasures all this time because he was disconnected from himself. In recovery, he has the opportunity to reconnect with his real self and can discover things about himself and his world that the addiction denied him.

At least the addict, in this phase of his recovery, keeps an open mind, and in so doing doesn't miss out on the signs of everyday life that alert him to another truth about himself. Sometimes that discovery is diametrically opposed to what he held while in the grips of his disease.

All bias and rigidity—all preconceived notions that the disease cultivates and stultifies in the life of the addict—are slowly but surely diffused in the experience of recovery. This phenomenon affords the addict all kinds of new experiences. It doesn't cheat him of all the possibilities that his being is made to explore and personalize. In fact, the sign of boredom at this phase of recovery is usually a call to the discovery of new interests, of a change in career, in relationships, or in some other area of life's unlimited arena.

In a word, the exciting element of this new life knows no boundaries. Discrimination, exclusion, have no more role to play. As a result, the life of the person becomes richer not only in possibilities, but in the actual discovery of the multiple talents and propensities that finally are unbound and unhampered by preconceived ideas and biased opinions.

Ultimately, this characteristic of excitement creates more

personal happiness because it opens the way to love—a love that is free, unbounded, not exclusive. It is a universal and a truer kind of love. For love of one thing and not another is still incomplete. What is essential is that love really is the key to happiness—the reason why we exist.

Another reason why the life of the recovering addict is increasingly exciting is that it is devoid of fear. This fearless life is based on the guarantees of recovery itself. The initial act of trust that is asked of the newcomer at the beginning of recovery is based on the certitude that life never fails. The assurance for the addict is that as long as he acts with the intention of bettering life and of maintaining it, he will never be caught holding the short end. This certitude affirms that he is priceless and the recipient of an irrevocable gift, the nature of which is success with never a possibility of failure as long as he continues to seek himself in truth and in reality.

At an open meeting of Alcoholics Anonymous (a meeting opened to the public) that I had the privilege of attending, I heard a person share the following: "I've had a real bad day! It started off with a real unpleasant encounter with my supervisor at work. She accused me of pilfering some office supplies. I must say that my relationship with her has been rocky for a few months now. But I was devastated, and I really don't know where all this is going to end. To make matters worse, I was mugged on the subway after that awful day at work. Fortunately, I wasn't hurt, but I lost all my credit cards, plus about fifty dollars that I was carrying."

Someone in attendance then raised his hand to speak and responded in this way: "Certainly, you have had your share of setbacks and disappointments for one day. But in the midst of all these failings, you can go home tonight and tell yourself before falling asleep that despite all the failures of the day, you yourself are not a failure. You didn't pick up a drink, and you have life . . . and life never fails."

Yes, the experience of recovery is free of fear, even fear of failure. And it is also one of growing excitement as long as the process is kept in motion. An added element of excitement comes from the learning experience that itself evolves from a close look and attention to one's feelings. In the past, the addict used drugs to quell feelings, to avoid the fear of the feeling that he had or could have. In recovery, the discovery and the awareness of the surfacing of one feeling or the other is a pure delight.

Feelings prove, first of all, that one is alive. More important, it is exciting to seek out the meaning of feelings as they surface in us at the provocation of a million and one events and people in our lives. Every movement of feeling is an indicator of "my" gift—of who "I" am. The exciting thing is to read into these indicators and become more and more able to integrate that knowledge. This process of integration guides the artist into making choices, thereby fashioning a life-style that expresses the unique kind of life that is waiting to take flesh.

In the disease, the addict was always buffeted by feelings and threatened by them. In recovery, the emergence of feelings—all of them, the good and the bad—is pregnant with possibilities. Feelings become the key to the knowledge of self and of one's path in life.

Finally, this is the stage of recovery where the excitement carries over into the varied fields of human activity open to the recovering addict. This is where the addict advances in the discovery of his place in the areas of vocation, of career, of religious involvement, of relationships. A whole vista of destinies and experiences awaits the addict.

I personally feel that all people with this disease are called in recovery to play a very distinct role in the world. By that, I don't necessarily mean that all will become famous men and women. But I do feel that each and every recovering addict has recovered for a very specific purpose. And one of the excitements of life in recovery is ultimately to find that purpose . . . to create it. The call of the artist! The wonderful love of the Creator to allow us to find it ourselves instead of giving it to us ready-made!

Finding one's place in life is well demonstrated by the recovery story of a Methodist minister who told me this story:

"When I first found recovery, I was in such a deteriorated state that I was incapable of returning to the ministry. At the suggestion of some AA friends, I set out to find myself a 'get-well' job—that is, a job that is relatively easy and low in stress. I went to a temporary agency and was hired as a clerk-typist.

"As time went on and as I got better, I began to think in terms of returning to the ministry. However, in my growth in recovery, I was able to be more honest with myself. I knew that I had no inclination to return to parish work. Yet I also knew that I wanted to be a minister. I had no inkling as to what form that ministry could possibly take.

"For almost two years, I remained in the dark, with life giving absolutely no sign or illumination as to what I should do. In the meantime, I kept believing and trusting that the "Power greater than myself" would enlighten me at the proper time.

"At the very moment that I began sharing with recovering friends that my faith was beginning to run dry and that I was beginning to despair of ever finding my way, I received a telephone call from a friend of mine who works in the field of addiction. He invited me to attend a lecture that he was sponsoring on the topic of cocaine and its effects in the workplace.

"Believe me, in the growing depression over my own situation, I had no desire to attend a lecture! What, I thought to myself, is a lecture going to do for me? But because he was a friend and was expressing a caring interest in me, I did attend.

"And thank God I did! The lecturer happened to be a man of the cloth—a Catholic priest, to be exact. He gave a stimulating talk. When I approached him and thanked him for the lecture, I just happened, automatically and with no forethought in mind, to ask him what parish church he was affiliated with. He told me that he had no particular church and that he worked full time with alcoholics and drug addicts. I couldn't believe my ears! Here was a priest who wasn't busy with traditional ministry! I again just coincidentally said to him that I was having a problem with knowing what to do as a minister now that I was in recovery. His reply came in the form of an invitation to have lunch with him.

"And lunch we did on the following Tuesday. To make a long story short, that lunchtime was the moment that life had reserved for me. It was in meeting this man that I found out that I was made to work with alcoholics and drug addicts as a minister—my occupation to this day. And what a rich ministry it has been for me!"

A LOVING JOURNEY

The journey of progression in recovery brings us to the experience of finally being able to function as the loving creatures we are meant to be.

First of all, the recovering addict experiences love in the form of love of self. True, the two most important Commandments are love of God and of neighbor. In the biblical context, self-love is not mentioned for a very good reason. It can be explained by the very nature of love itself. To speak of loving anybody supposes love of self. One can only give what one has. And to be able to love God or neighbor, of necessity, one must love self.

And so, in the new experience of life in recovery, the addict learns to love self. It is a new experience for the addict, who, nine times out of ten, picked up in the course of his upbringing that to do something for oneself is to be selfish. Here, the addict learns the difference between selfishness and self-love. Selfishness, of course, is wrong. It robs the human being of happiness because it is destructive. It makes one unappealing, and inevitably leads to loneliness and isolation. Self-love, on the other hand, is doing something for oneself, and it is not destructive. As a result, for the first time in his life perhaps, the addict enjoys the right and duty to put himself first. He can because, in matters of living, if someone does something that is not good first of all for self, it can't do any good for anyone else.

To have recovered the right to love of self is a release that gives motivation to living. In the area of love, more awaits the recovering addict. He is now able to establish relationships that have some hope of health and survival. Now, the addict brings something to the relationship. He brings himself, which is a gift that keeps growing with every phase of development that the addict experiences.

No more is there a vague and indistinct cloud between sex and relationship. The recovering addict has a better grasp of the role of sex in his life, and the distinction between where sex ends and where relationship begins. He realizes that a relationship is a spiritual connection with another human being.

Now, more spiritual than he ever was before, he can respond to relationships. As a result, he seeks them out. If they fail, again the addict has become richer through a greater knowledge of himself, of his peers, and of the world that is now his to conquer and to enliven.

Finally, the experience of life in recovery is a loving journey because it leads to the service of others. There is something essentially altruistic in the character and temperament of the addict. In fact, one of the symptoms of the disease is the ability on the part of the active addict to take responsibility for the lives of others at the expense of his own. In addiction, this trait is manipulative and destructive of others. Now, the addict can with no loss to himself be a positive force in the lives of others. As a result, not a few recovering addicts find employment in the service fields. Others volunteer some of their free time for one or the other numerous organizations that bring solace and help to human pain. You see, the addict is an expert in human pain. He has suffered the only pain that has no name because it is so beyond the human word. That is why this aspect of the recovery is an opportunity for the addict to relieve the pain in others. It can be in the form of assistance in soothing the physical, mental, or spiritual pain of the less fortunate.

Whatever the nature of the help offered, it is clear that the recovering addict has a role to play. Life wants to communicate itself. The healthier and the more alive the addict becomes, the more the addict wants to contribute what he can to those human beings still suffering from human pain.

A recovering addict of three years was prompted by her friends in Narcotics Anonymous to begin helping the newcomers who popped into the meeting rooms almost daily. She told me one day that it was only when she began speaking to the new members of the group and spending some time sharing her own experience with them that she began to feel more alive herself.

"It was," she confided, "as if my desire for sobriety and clean living was made stronger and more appealing. I was experiencing what they had been telling me right along: 'You keep it by giving it away.' Now I find myself more disposed to seeing my life less in terms of a job and a career as in my role in being there for other people in the measure that they want what I, in my little way, have to give."

A HUMBLE JOURNEY

If the experience of recovery from the disease of addiction makes life creative, exciting, and loving, it also adds to it a dimension of humbleness. Only the tall man can bend lower than the short man. It is strange and paradoxical that, wherever one encounters greatness, right alongside of it one finds humility. The creature destined to dominate the world is the most vulnerable and weakest of all creatures. And here we have life—a recovery of a life. In the measure that the real life surfaces, comes forth, and becomes real, it is accompanied by an experience, or rather another reality, we call humility or humbleness.

Humility is the part of the journey that tells the recovering addict how to go about traveling through life. It is the map of the trip, the road signs, the instructions. It is, in brief, the condition without which we can't make spiritual progress, without which we can't make progress in life and in living.

Life is humble because it is honest and real. That is why, in addiction, there is so much arrogance. There is no reality or truth in addiction. Consequently, there is no humility, either. True humility as an ingredient of life can only be found in the *real*.

Not surprisingly, the recovering addict finds humility in prayer and meditation. Prayer is the place where he talks to God, to his Higher Power, whatever that might be for each individual addict. It is the place where he can be the most honest without embarrassment or fear of reprisal. No one needs to cover up the truth in prayer. When one cannot be honest with someone for lack of courage, one can always be honest in prayer and keep alive the current of truth, which is in itself life-giving. In fact, prayer is the place of all places where all is truth and where fantasy has no role. Prayer is humble because it is in essence the exercise of acceptance of the real as it is—good or bad—and of gratitude for the real. To be accepting is already to begin to be grateful. It is the first seed of love.

The journey of recovery is humble because it is eternal. By eternal, I mean it is never lost, and it is time-consuming. In fact, it is so time-consuming that it is unending. Growth in life, as we said before, has no limit—no ceiling. It goes on and on. It is eternal and infinite. It is a gift given for all time and beyond.

Finally, the journey of recovery is humble because it deals with the present moment, the rich "now." How, you might ask, can the "now" moment in the human being's life be humble? Most of our days are filled with unmeaningful things, events, people, and circumstances. In the days of active addiction, the person addicted would try to escape these "now" moments, which were dull and seemingly void of any possibility of expanding life, by taking drugs. In recovery, the addict learns that it is in these "now" moments, which in themselves are rather ordinary and even dull, that he will find the source and the resource for the greater things in life that he really seeks.

In spiritual matters, the "more" always comes from the "less." Better to be in the "dull now," which is real and alive, than in the "brilliant future," which is pure fantasy and totally unreal.

Thousands of examples forthcoming from recovering people attest to the fact that because they were sober—that is, present to the "now," the reality of the present moment in their lives—they met the person and had the experience that was to usher them on their way into the very destiny of their lives. That life *is* the miracle finally becomes meaningful.

10

The
Mystery
of
Mysteries

IT WOULD SEEM that we have come to the end of the journey of recovery. And, in a sense, we have. But in another real sense, we have not, since recovery from addiction is without end. The physical recovery and the mental recovery are somewhat limited. The recovery of physical health and of mental sanity can go so far. But the spiritual recovery is without ceiling, without confinement, and open to a limitlessness that goes beyond even our wildest imaginings.

Yes, the journey of recovery is, in a sense, over. The addict has recovered his physical and mental well-being. Also, he has recovered his gift . . . his connection with life. That is what is meant when it is said that he has "spiritually" come to life.

Having returned to life, he finds himself launched into the very movement or process of life itself. For certain, he has reached his destination—his proper place in life. But the very nature of that place compels him to function as he was born to function. He begins to love. The gift of recovering his life—a mystery in itself—ejects him into the place of love, the unending journey, the mystery of mysteries.

When I was a young child, my mother often relaxed from her housework by playing the piano. One particularly warm August afternoon, I was standing next to my mother at the piano. She was singing these words from a well-known song: "Ah, sweet mystery of life, at last I found you." It caught my full attention, and I waited to hear the words of the next verse: "Yes, 'tis love and love alone the world is seeking. . . ." I was immediately reassured and felt that I had just discovered the secret of living. "Of course," I said to myself, "if you want your life to go well, you have to love." I was elated! Little did I know that from the mystery that life surely is, I had been led into the very eye of the mystery . . . into what I call once again the mystery of mysteries.

The addict in his quest of recovery from addiction experiences an analogous phenomenon. After having traveled the hard, at times baffling, road of recovery, he finds himself not with an answer but with a greater mystery still. He is faced with the job of going out into his world and being the loving person that he was destined to be.

For this reason, I should say a few words about love—the place where recovery brings the addict—the place that we are meant to be as we answer "yes" to the call of life, to the experience of maturity itself.

Once in the place of love, the human being is left with no choice. He finds himself in a totally powerless world. He must be totally powerless himself—totally noncontrolling as he passes the threshold of love and enters into its deeper chambers.

One of the fatal mistakes that we often make in life is to attempt to know love—to dissect it, to control it so that we can be sure of it. Shakespeare's plays are wonderful demonstrations of that truth, *Romeo and Juliet* is a superb statement in art form of the tragedy that results when one seeks to control love.

In fact, the whole play is an attempt on the part of the protagonists to know each other's love and to express it in just terms to one another so that they may live secure in that love.

Without a doubt, *Romeo and Juliet* is a play that has the basic ingredient needed to be a true tragedy. After all, the protagonists die at the end. Yet *Romeo and Juliet* is not a tragedy. It lacks the breadth and scope of life itself. A tragedy, even in death, allows the audience a glimpse into the wonder of life both from within and from without. In *Romeo and Juliet,* the view is lifeless and full of regret. In their pursuit of love, the hero and heroine lose their love. And the loss is brought about by some "star-crossed" coincidence, an unfortunate series of events, a misreading of the reality that is taking place. In a word, the loss of each other in death is provoked by an error of judgment—the very control that was supposed to assure and guarantee the survival of their love.

Compare *Romeo and Juliet* to Shakespeare's later play *Antony and Cleopatra.* This latter play is also about two people in love. But they are older and more mature. And so is their love, which they never question. They accept it and live it. In addiction, the constant attempt to make the other "know" that he or she is loved becomes, in this play, irrelevant and obsolete.

As a result, the play ends with the death of the lovers. It is not a death due to accident and fortuitous circumstance. It is not a death due to something less than they. It is a death into greater life. At the end of the play, their world becomes too small. Shakespeare says that Antony's pockets become islands. When he takes a step, he goes from continent to continent. Cleopatra, as she puts the poison viper to her breast, exclaims, "I have immortal longings in me" (Act V, Scene 2).

No, the death of Antony and Cleopatra is not the result of a mistake or of a lesser event. Rather, it is a requirement of their love, which, left unquestioned, grows beyond the limits of the planet and cries out for other worlds in order to expand and grow still more.

Love, by its very nature, defies knowledge and control. To the addict—to all of us at this point in growth—the fear of not being loved is horrendous. Therefore, the addict, as well as all of us, seeks reassurance from the loved one. But love is the mystery of mysteries. It plays only in mystery and not in sureness, in controllable terrain. To want to put it there is to risk missing the point—the very point that is the goal of the quest. And the love dies, not from expansion but from restriction.

Many object with cries of "What do I do?" and "Not *knowing* that I am loved, how do I handle the ensuing emptiness?" The answer is at once simple and awesome. Feel the emptiness, embrace it, make love to it. In the very connection with the real emptiness, in the honest and painful acceptance of it, love is now free to move. It is now free to come in and fill the void. What a miracle! It is similar to the miracle of life itself. For what is life if not the sudden eruption of something more from something less? Creation, in the Judeo-Christian context, is the making of something from nothing. On the other hand,

Darwinism sees creation differently. Yet the selective process inherent to the theory of evolution also results in the higher creature evolving from the lesser one. It is the story of the barren womb producing the newborn child, of the insignificant seed giving forth the magnificent and gigantic tree.

So, too, with love. To say yes to the emptiness is to release the very process by which I become gifted with the greater truth. In this case, it is the gift of gifts. It is love.

Love is a reflection of the very nature of humankind. And it follows that the very measure of a human being is taken from his capacity to love . . . and from literally nothing else—not from his riches, his prestige, or his accomplishments. In other words, love is the only full-blooded human act. As a result, it is when he loves that man achieves his full stature as the moral creature that he is. It is when he loves that his action most fully reflects the mystery that he is—not only as a human being but as the individual and unique human being that he is. It is when I love that I am most "me."

Being love, I am necessarily gift. And that is why I am most myself when I love, because only then do I offer the perfect gift—the best of what I have to give. It is the gift of myself—of my spirit. More than my word, more than my services gladly rendered, the gift of self is the most humble, the least pretentious, because it is the most real. It is a gift from the inside out.

What a wonderful discovery. To find out that not only am I worth something, but that I am the most worthy of all that exists! First of all, even if something other is greater—and no doubt there is—of what value would it be to me if *I* were not there?

But there is more. If love makes of my emptiness—in fact, originally my nothingness—the perfect gift, it is also the underlying substance of my very existence. I like to say that it is the oxygen of my spiritual lungs. It is why we, as human beings, live. Love gives life and maintains it throughout space and time. In fact, without love, I die. Therein lies the hope of the alcoholic and the drug addict. Therein lies the hope of all of us endowed with human life. Now, we can understand the pain that is the addict's when the disease in its progression gives him the experience of not being loved by anyone. For the person caged by the disease of addiction, even the love of the people who he *knows* love him offers him little consolation. He always knows at the same time that if those same people really knew him, they would condemn him and give him their backs.

"And why is this?" one may ask. The answer is very simple. When I allow myself to be disconnected from the reality of life, I cannot love. I cease to be there—to be present to the reality of myself. I become disconnected from my very self. As a result, I cannot live my gift. It becomes impossible for me to love. You see, I am no longer "me."

It is not difficult to understand the intrinsic and ultimate evil of addiction. The disease destroys man's capacity to love. And more than that, it goes on to lie to the addict and to tell him that he is not loved and that he can't love in return. This is the real cause and nature of that unspeakable pain that is the lot of all addicted people. To be made to love and to be incapable of loving. Truly, it is the pain of hell itself. There exists in the annals of human experience no greater pain. It is worse than dying. It is to be dead alive. There is great truth in the often-heard description of the alcoholic and the drug addict as the "living dead." It is no wonder then that at a given point in the disease the addict wants to die. Once again, better to be dead than to be dead alive.

In fact, to die with love is not to die. That, in part, is the message of the play *Antony and Cleopatra*. Dying with love, both protagonists embrace death as the passageway to a greater and more expansive life. Of course, "To die with love is not to die" is a paradox. One can only begin to perceive its meaningfulness when one sees humankind as a gift—a creation of love. If the human being is a gift, then he most surely will find his greatest expression in the ultimate giving—that is, the total surrender. Therein lies the truth inherent in dying. If we refuse to die, how can we realize our full potential as beings of gift and of love? It is only in the act of dying that we stand a chance not only to remain ourselves but to become more of who we are . . . precisely by giving all of it up.

Finally, this gift of love works miracles. Once I love, I have in hand the most effective tool for righting the wrong. To live in love is to be free of even our regretful escapades of the past. I say that because as soon as I recover the reality of who I am—of the fact that I am love—*that* love goes to work and begins the healing process to whomever hurt and pain were given. That is why the recovering addict need not worry in his early days of recovery about repairing the damage that he, as a diseased person, certainly has inflicted on his loved ones. Of course, he will *want* to satisfy the urgings of his mind and of his emotions by immediately wanting to take charge of the repair work. But no need! Love is already operative again in his life, it works even at a distance. In the same way, his family was hurting while he was active even when he was physically separated from them and not at home; so, too, now that he is in recovery, the love in him that gives life through space and time will immediately be life-giving to them—the suffering codependents. Later, when the addict is more fully whole and in life, it will be wise to approach in a more physical and felt way the ones in his life whom he always loved "not wisely, but too well."

In this context, we must recognize that the first act of love for the victim of addiction is to admit powerlessness over the drug to save *his* life. Furthermore, he soon enough comes to realize that by extending his surrender—his gift—and admitting powerlessness over all things, he preserves *all* of life.

It is true for all people. The key to the mystery of life is undoubtedly found in love. For only when they allow the process of love to take place and they surrender—give their all—are they ushered into the realm of their true destiny—that of being heirs to the kingdom. It is only in that act of unconditional gift that they, too, become the divine—the recipients of the promise—the sons and daughters of God.

11

A Short Conclusion

ADDICTION, to me, is a call to life identical to the experience of being born. At birth, Nature in her loving relationship with us answers a whole and decisive yes to the invitation of life. In addiction, we answer for ourselves. If the answer is no, we continue on the path of the living dead. If we say yes, we recover our lives, the gift of gifts, and we grow.

The disease of addiction is not a physical, mental, and spiritual disease. It is much more a spiritual disease—a disease of life—with various components attached to it. These components are physical, mental, psychological, social, financial—the list is unending.

Nothing is left untouched once this disease establishes itself in the human spirit. It's a disconnection from within that with time effects a disconnection with everything that the diseased person touches and loves.

I said very little throughout this book of what we now call codependents—the family and friends of the addicted person. Yet these wonderful people are present throughout. Since this is a spiritual disease, the method of transmission is also spiritual. It is transmitted through love.

The spouse, the lover, the child, the parent, the relative, and the friend do not need to have a physical contact with the disease or with the diseased person. To become a codependent, all that one needs is to have a loving relationship, a caring relationship, with the addict.

In fact, it is my experience that the codependent's pain is greater still than that of the physical alcoholic and drug addict. It is greater because it is all spiritual, and therefore deeper. Another significant factor that maximizes the pain is that the codependent finds no relief from it. The alcoholic and the drug addict can always get high, and in that fashion experience temporary respite from the pain.

The codependents of this world have, without a doubt, "paid their dues." As a result, they, more so maybe than the addicts themselves, have a right to recovery. Efforts to procure treatment for the families and friends of addicts are being made. We can only hope that opportunities of treatment for them become greater still.

In closing, I would be remiss if I didn't make a statement for the economically distressed and for the minorities, in particular for the Hispanic people. If our society is to become more human and loving, we must find some way to offer treatment in a caring and effective way to those who can't afford it and to those who can only receive it in their native tongue.

One thing is sure. Caring attention to the treatment of this disease will contribute to the preservation of the addict's life. At the same time, it will turn a sometimes sick and tarnished world to health and brilliant gold.

Blessed are the addicts . . .